THE FREEDOM CENTER JOURNAL

The Freedom Center Journal is published twice a year and is based at the University of Cincinnati College of Law, P.O. Box 210040, Cincinnati, OH 45221-0040.

ISBN: 978-0-9819178-3-2

This special issue was designed by Stan Brod's Fall 2010 Design Methodology Class at the University of Cincinnati College of Design, Architecture, Art and Planning.

Individuals and Institutions interested in subscribing to the *Freedom Center Journal* may do so by sending an email to UCLawFCJ@gmail.com.

Domestic Price $30 per volume (2 issues); $18 per individual issue
Non-U.S. Price: $35 per volume (2 issues); $20 per individual issue
Special Edition Price: $30 for non-subscribers

For information on submissions, please visit our website at: http://www.law.uc.edu/institutes-centers/rgsj/fcj/subguide.

THE FREEDOM CENTER JOURNAL

2010 — 2011

THE ROSENTHAL INSTITUTE FOR JUSTICE /

OHIO INNOCENCE PROJECT

Director	Mark Godsey
Staff Attorneys	Jennifer Paschen Bergeron Karla Markley Hall Carrie Wood
Administrative Coordinator & Policy Analyst	Jodi Shorr
Fellows 2010–2011	Nicole Billec Molly CaJacob Guy Cardamone Andrew Cleves Megan Collard Jen Coy Lauren Creditt Kayla Delk Zach El-Sawaf Lindsey Fleissner Claire Gutmann Nathan Henegar Julie Kathman Jessica Lantaff Sean Martz Hilly McGahan Ryan McGraw Dominique Mix Angela Neyer Amanda Rieger

This issue is dedicated to those who have been wrongfully convicted. The proceeds from this issue will be used to assist exonerees in a manner determined by the Innocence Network Board of Directors.

We wish to offer special thanks to **Lois and Dick Rosenthal** whose generous support made this project possible. Their dedication to both artistic expression and social reform, including fighting the injustice of wrongful conviction, continues to positively impact our community in immeasurable ways.

The *Freedom Center Journal* would also like to thank **Ann and Harry Santen** for their continued support of the Journal.

THE FREEDOM CENTER JOURNAL
ILLUSTRATED TRUTH / *EXPRESSIONS OF WRONGFUL CONVICTION*
Volume 2, Issue 2 / Fall 2010

CONTENTS

LETTER FROM THE EDITOR

Teresa Martinez-Molwane 16

PREFACE

Mark Godsey 19
Professor of Law and Director of the Rosenthal Institute for Justice / Ohio Innocence Project
Daniel P. and Judith L. Carmichael Professor of Law

INTRODUCTION *On Innocence and Lawlessness*

Adrian Parr 21
Associate Professor in the Department of Women's Gender and Sexuality Studies
and the School of Architecture and Interior Design at the University of Cincinnati

PART ONE *Resurrected* by Dan Bolick
Works photographed by Scott Van Kirk

Dan Bright 28
Gregory Bright 30
Albert Burrell 32
Clyde Charles 34
Clarence Elkins 36
Michael Graham 38
Curtis Kyles 40
Ryan Matthews 42
Robert McClendon 44
Nancy Smith 46
John Thompson 48
Drew Whitley 50
Calvin Willis 52

PART TWO *Expressions of the Wrongfully Convicted*

Written and researched by the 2010—2011 *Freedom Center Journal* Associate Members and the Ohio Innocence Project Fellows

Works photographed by Sean Hughes, Lisa Haynes-Henry, and Sam Spencer

Steven Barnes........56
Levon Brooks........60
Darryl Burton........62
Keith Bush........68
Al Cleveland........72
Chris Conover........76
Dwayne Allen Dail........82
Gary Drinkard........84
Clarence Elkins........88
R. Dean Gillispie........94
Jeffrey Scott Hornoff........100
Timothy Howard........108
Lee Wayne Hunt........114
Ron Keine........118
Gloria Killian........122
Ray Krone........128
Larry Lamb........132
Walter Lomax........134
Bill Macumber........138
Robert McClendon........142
Beverly Monroe........146
Mike Piaskowski........152
Atif Rafay........154
Julie Rea........172
Kalvin Michael Smith........176
Nancy Smith........180
Raymond Towler........184
Sherman Townsend........190

/ Contents continued on next page

PART THREE *The Innocents* by Taryn Simon

Photos and interviews by Taryn Simon

Reprinted with permission of Umbrage Printing

Warith Habib Abdal 196
A.B. Butler 198
Clyde Charles 200
Charles Fain 202
Paula Gray 204
William Gregory 206
Ronald Jones 208
Larry Mayes 210
Anthony Robinson 212
Calvin Washington 214
Ron Williamson 216

REFERENCES & ACKNOWLEDGEMENTS

References 219
Acknowledgements 224

The works appearing in this issue will be on public display at the National Underground Railroad Freedom Center in Cincinnati, Ohio, from April 7, 2011 until July 9, 2011.

The exhibit will open on April 7, 2011 in conjunction with the 2011 Innocence Network Conference hosted by the Rosenthal Institute for Justice / Ohio Innocence Project at the University of Cincinnati College of Law.

LETTER FROM THE EDITOR

TERESA MARTINEZ-MOLWANE
Editor in Chief

When Mark Godsey, Director, Rosenthal Institute for Justice/Ohio Innocence Project (OIP) at the University of Cincinnati College of Law, approached the *Freedom Center Journal* (FCJ) regarding working together on a project for the 2011 Innocence Network Conference, we were honored and excited about the possibilities. Professor Godsey proposed that we dedicate a future issue of the FCJ to the creative expressions of individuals who had been convicted of crimes which they did not commit. As a journal that prides itself for truly being interdisciplinary, we welcomed the opportunity to work with the OIP while also bringing awareness to the social injustices experienced by those who have been wrongfully convicted.

Following our initial discussions about this special issue, the project evolved and grew from a 100 page book with a color insert to the art book that is presented here. The collaborations that made this issue what it is soon expanded beyond the law school to multiple departments across the University of Cincinnati (UC) campus. At the McMicken College of Arts and Sciences, Professor Sean Hughes' photojournalism students photographed the works that appear in Part II of the issue. At UC's renowned College of Design, Art, Architecture, and Planning (DAAP), fifth-year students in Professor Stan Brod's Fall 2010 Design Methodology Studio designed the layout of the entire issue, as well as its cover. We are sincerely grateful to Professors Hughes and Brod and their students for helping us to realize the vision of this project. Additionally, Professor Adrian Parr, who holds joint appointments in the Department of Women's Gender and Sexuality Studies and the School of Architecture and Interior Design and who has written extensively on art's impact on politics, provided the Introduction to this special issue.

It is particularly fitting that this collaborative issue of the FCJ is the first issue to have been published since the October 2010 launch of the Center for Race, Gender, and Social Justice at UC's College of Law of which FCJ is formally a part. By building coalitions with organizations locally, nationally, and globally, the Center seeks to identify the interconnectedness of what justice means across disciplines and communities. In helping to give voice to the wrongfully convicted, this collaboration between FCJ, OIP, and other colleges and departments across the UC campus does just that.

This issue is divided into three sections. Part I includes work from Dan Bolick's "Resurrected" collection of portraits. Bolick's paintings depict individuals who were wrongfully convicted and sentenced to death or to life in prison. His work has traveled the country and will be on exhibit, along with the other works in the book, at the National Underground Railroad Freedom Center in Cincinnati, Ohio, from April 7, 2011 to July 9, 2011. The exhibit was curated by Professor Laura Stewart's Spring 2011 Exhibition Planning and Design class at DAAP.

Part II of this issue consists of the creative expression of twenty-eight individuals who also were wrongfully convicted. Each individual's work is accompanied by a case profile that includes biographical information about the individual artist. Not all of the artists included in this section have been exonerated. Some have been released from prison without an official recognition of wrongful conviction; some still remain in prison irrespective of their actual innocence.

The case profiles were researched by OIP Fellows and written by FCJ Associate Members. The profiles were compiled from newspaper articles, media interview transcripts, various website sources, case opinions and other court documents, and personal knowledge provided by attorneys or others who personally have advocated on behalf of these individuals. Some stories have been reprinted with permission of various innocence network organizations across the country whose students, staff, and faculty worked on the cases. The profiles illustrate common factors that lead to wrongful convictions, including inadequate legal representation, police and prosecutorial misconduct, perjured testimony, mistaken eyewitness testimony, racial prejudice, and community and political pressure to solve a case. Whatever the cause of the wrongful conviction, the result remains the same: innocent people are being incarcerated for many years, some sentenced to life, and some sentenced to death, for crimes they did not commit.

Part III of this issue includes a portion of Taryn Simon's nationally touring photography exhibit, "The Innocents," which portrays individuals who were wrongfully convicted, incarcerated, and later exonerated through DNA evidence. Through her work, Simon demonstrates how photography is used to wrongfully convict innocent people across race, gender, and class lines. Simon's photographs are accompanied by interviews she conducted with those who were wrongfully convicted.

This special collaborative issue of the FCJ represents several months of hard work on the part of many students, faculty, and staff. On behalf of the Freedom Center Journal, I would like to thank OIP Administrative Coordinator and Policy Analyst Jodi Shorr and OIP Fellow Amanda Rieger (UC Law Class of 2012) for cataloging and organizing all of the works in this issue; and Professor

Emily Houh, our Faculty Advisor, and Sherry English, Director of Relations for the College of Law, for all of their guidance during the course of this project.

Finally, we would like to thank Professor Godsey for recognizing the *Freedom Center Journal* as the appropriate forum for illustrating the extraordinary experiences of the artists and subjects featured in this issue. We are honored to be a part of OIP's inspired work and to make this work available and accessible to a larger audience. Though a relatively small gesture, we hope that this special issue appropriately honors the convicted innocent for their great courage and humanity.

Teresa Martinez-Molwane
Editor in Chief

PREFACE

MARK GODSEY
Director, Rosenthal Institute for Justice/Ohio Innocence Project
Daniel P. and Judith L. Carmichael Professor of Law

One of my most prized possessions is the painting *As Long As There is One* by my long-time client and close friend Roger "Dean" Gillispie (p. 97). Dean, who, at the time of this writing, is still in prison after nearly two decades for crimes he did not commit, painted this image of a warrior to motivate me leading up to the first post-conviction innocence hearing that was scheduled in his case back in July 2008. Ever since then, it has hung on the wall outside of my bedroom at home; it is the first thing I see when I walk out of my room each morning to start the day. Although I didn't need motivation to prepare for Dean's hearing, seeing the painting and reading the inscription Dean wrote for it has inspired me on many occasions to overcome the exhaustion and burnout inherent in a line of work that has such steep, uphill battles every day.

Since Dean gave me the painting in the Spring of 2008, it has seen me through the exonerations of Robert McClendon (p. 142), Nancy Smith (p. 180), and Raymond Towler (p. 184). It has also helped me through innumerable defeats and setbacks, including a series of particularly heartbreaking losses in Dean's case. But with Dean, Robert, Nancy, and Raymond, I noticed what others in this line of work have noticed as well—that the pain and frustration of wrongful conviction and incarceration often manifests itself in incredibly meaningful forms of artistic expression. The wrongfully convicted have important things to say, and it is clear that art is a particularly powerful and effective way for them to say it.

The efforts of these Ohio Innocence Project clients gave me the idea to collect various forms of expression from those who were wrongfully convicted throughout the United States and put them in one location and in one publication to share with others. The works appearing in this issue will be on public display at the National Underground Railroad Freedom Center in Cincinnati, Ohio, from April 7, 2011 until July 9, 2011. The exhibit is called *Illustrated Truth: Expressions of Wrongful Conviction*. Lois and Dick Rosenthal, who, through their generosity, make the work of the Ohio Innocence Project possible, also made this publication and the exhibit possible through the support of their foundation.

The individuals who contributed to Part II: Expressions of the Wrongfully Convicted, are primarily individuals who have been exonerated and cleared of all charges for which they were wrongfully convicted. However, similar to my experience with Dean, many of us who work in this field have clients who we believe are innocent but who have not yet been vindicated and released. Many of these inmates, like Dean, have produced powerful expressions of wrongful conviction through art. Thus, I encouraged attorneys working with Innocence Network organizations to submit the artistic expressions of their current clients—not yet exonerated—for whom a colorable claim of actual innocence exists, and for whom the attorney representing the artist has developed a strong belief in the client's actual innocence.

In the spirit of UC/2019, this issue and exhibit are the products of interdisciplinary collaboration. Photojournalism students working with Professor Sean Hughes at UC's McMicken College of Arts and Sciences volunteered their time to photograph all the works that appear in Part II of this issue. Undergraduate students in Professor Stan Brod's Fall 2010 Design Methodology Studio at UC's College of Design, Art, Architecture and Planning (DAAP) did all of the wonderful design work and layout that you see in the following pages. Dr. Adrian Parr, Associate Professor in the Department of Women's Gender and Sexuality Studies and the School of Architecture and Interior Design at UC, provided the Introduction for the issue, and DAAP Professor Laura Stewart's Exhibition Planning and Design class designed the physical exhibit that will run at the National Underground Railroad Freedom Center in 2011. The staff of the *Freedom Center Journal*, a joint publication of the UC College of Law and the National Underground Railroad Freedom Center, took the lead with all of the hard work it took to put this publication together. Third-year law student and Editor in Chief, Teresa Martinez-Molwane, and Professor and Faculty Advisor to the Journal, Emily Houh, in particular, carried the laboring oar. From the Ohio Innocence Project, Jodi Shorr and especially second-year student Amanda Rieger put in countless hours collecting and organizing the many elements that comprise this issue and exhibit. Many thanks to all of them for their important roles in making this come together.

I hope that you are inspired and motivated by the works in this issue the way that Dean's painting *As Long As There is One* continues to inspire and motivate me as I, like many others, struggle to undo the injustices of wrongful conviction.

Mark Godsey
Director, Rosenthal Institute for Justice/Ohio Innocence Project
Daniel P. and Judith L. Carmichael Professor of Law

INTRODUCTION

"On Innocence and Lawlessness"

ADRIAN PARR

What do we mean when we speak of innocence? It could be a time in a person's life, such as childhood. Or, even a state: childishness. For some it refers to character traits of inexperience and naivety. It commonly signifies purity. But more than anything it is an attitude to life: trust. When considered in this way, the concept of innocence seems incompatible with the experiences we are called upon to witness as part of the *Illustrated Truth: Expressions of Wrongful Conviction*. This exhibition presents the appalling effects of wrongful conviction and the subsequent fortitude to uphold the claim to innocence despite the failure of the Law to do justice and more importantly the subjugation of a life under the Law.

The words and images that make up the testimonies, stories, and memories gathered throughout this exhibition and issue introduce a fundamental failure at the level of society and the judicial system. They present a moment when the innocent become the victims of society. Of a Law that has turned into a dogmatic image of thought, to borrow from French philosopher Gilles Deleuze. That is, when the Law loses touch with the creative moment of doing law and succumbs to the arbitrary forces of rules. The works on display reveal the violence of the Law, as it criminalizes a body. And as the body is inscribed as a felon, lawless, and an immoral entity, it is forever changed. In this way the juridical moment is at its core the instantiation of a political relation because it arbitrates over, designates, situates, and organizes the potential of bodies.

The realm of aesthetics is especially well positioned to activate and articulate the political condition. As Jacques Rancière outlined in *The Politics of Aesthetics*, it is at the level of sensation and affect where the explosive potential of aesthetics lies. Redistributing the sensible, aesthetics interrupts how language usually circulates throughout the social field, organizing bodies into specific roles and distributing them throughout the social field according to these roles. Art, that is, reconfigures what can be said and how it can be said. By engaging the sensorial imaginative body and putting it to work in unconventional ways, art can radically change how reality is ordered. It does this by interrupting moral norms, stereotypes, and opinions at the level of corporeal sense, introducing into the visible and audible sphere of normative social space otherwise unspeakable and invisible dimensions.

Illustrated Truth addresses an unrecognizable moment, one that is produced when innocence collides with an act of betrayal from within the order of the Law. The feelings and emotions that emerge out of this betrayal transform our sense of security in the Law, rendering it vulnerable despite its authority. In this respect the exhibition marks a political moment. Indeed, it is not so much that the meaning of the lawless body interrupts the Law; rather it is the innocent body that challenges the Law and in so doing places it under pressure so that the lawlessness inherent in the Law is exposed. Lawlessness here is understood as a political will, and this is the very subject matter of the innocence movement on the whole.

There is an important difference between doing justice to the Law as an abstract construct and an exercise in practical reasoning, and that of creating laws that do justice to a situation. All the works in this exhibition are a call to the latter as they do not denounce the Law. On the contrary, all those whose work is represented here call on it in all its fallibility and they place their trust in it. The call itself recognizes that jurisprudence is a contact sport because it directly engages with and is activated by the material realities of the citizen-body. What we as spectators are in effect witnessing is an appeal to the Law to revisit and right the wrongs of an unjust decision. And through the witness the Law trembles in the face of its own lawlessness.

It is not enough to say that an unjust legal decision negates the Law. Rather, the unjust decision needs to be embraced, challenged, and tested for the legal problem it poses. It is this encounter with the Law-as-creative problem where the material vitality of doing law springs to life. And as such, the very system of practicing law is infused with compassion for its silenced victims. It is at this juncture where instrumental reason is affected by sentiment and the perforation that ensues fills the Law with political force once more, pushing it in the direction of ethics and away from the ills of moralizing.

Releasing people who are innocent from jail will not change the wrongs they have endured. It will never bring back time. But it will restore respect and dignity to both the individual and society, fusing the two so as to render community sensible. And moreover, it is an act of justice in the purest sense of the term. That is justice as a transformative moment in time, when the scabs of past wounds crack open the present to produce new directions and hope for the future once more. It is a moment when the present is transformed by the archival secrets of the past, such as those that lie within DNA and other empirical traces, and by the desires of the social field from which legal adjudication emerges.

These artworks are a political act in so far as they change our perception and feelings toward the 'inmate', the 'murderer', or the 'person on death row'. The otherwise nameless, and sometimes forgotten people of the innocence movement who are all brought to life through the aesthetics of sensation and affect. *Illustrated Truth* brings these previously silenced and invisible bodies back into the body politic to be heard and seen again, with a view to producing tangible change. Last but not least, the exhibition is a celebration of a pivotal political act: when the legal subject transforms into a political subject.

Adrian Parr
Associate Professor in the Department of Women's Gender and Sexuality Studies and the School of Architecture and Interior Design at the University of Cincinnati

PART I ⁄ RESURRECTED BY **DAN BOLICK**

Imagine, if you can, *what it must feel like to have the state take your life. Now imagine what it must feel like knowing that you are INNOCENT of the crime that you have been condemned for doing! To the human beings depicted in "Resurrected" it was their daily reality. I don't want the viewer to be able to escape the gaze of the people in these paintings and drawings...I want the viewer to see anger, bitterness, hope, acceptance, salvation and ultimate resurrection. What happened to these unfortunate people is intolerable. Wrongful convictions happen everyday. It should not be accepted.*

– Dan Bolick

DAN BOLICK

I was a career Art teacher for the inner-city Pittsburgh Public Schools for many years. Thirty-four to be exact. It is an accomplishment of which I am very proud. During that time, I worked with many youths who wound up on the wrong side of the law. Some were killed. Some got caught up in the legal system and found themselves being accused of petty crimes they hadn't committed. After being gone from my class for a while they would return asking "Why me?" I tried to explain to them that the criminal justice system is not always fair, is somewhat broken, and is simply best to be avoided. I would tell them that sometimes the easy people to blame get fingered for crimes they didn't commit.

The same kids would often get into trouble over and over again. They were caught up in a vicious cycle and their crimes escalated as their anger over their situations increased. During my final few years of teaching, I saw more angry students than ever before. As the anger level increased, the school became a physically unsafe place to work. Student on student assaults escalated. Student on faculty assaults escalated. A culture of anger and fear dominated daily life. Eventually the anger was directed at me. The teaching of art, which I had loved so much, became very difficult. Simply trying to maintain order required 110% of my energy. I decided that it was time to retire from the classroom.

I became a full-time painter. The first thing I did was to attempt to paint the anger that I had lived with so closely during my final years of teaching. The end result was a series of portrait paintings, which I called "The Young Urban Warrior Portraits." Painting these portraits was a cathartic experience for me. Eventually, on the strength of these paintings, I was given the opportunity to have a solo exhibition of new paintings at The Westmoreland Museum of American Art in Greensburg, Pennsylvania.

But what to paint? Having removed myself from the classroom and having painted the angry portraits eliminated the tension that I had felt. I wanted to paint something that could help people. I wanted to create socially responsible art.

Remembering my students, I decided to focus on the wrongfully convicted. I wanted to increase the awareness of ordinary citizens to this terrible problem in our society. Sometimes the role of an artist can be that of the people's conscience. I wanted to create art that was not supposed to be entertaining to the viewer. I wanted to create art that was confrontational. Painful realities tend to become invisible for most people. I wanted to give a visual voice to the problem of wrongful incarceration. Hopefully my art could act as a mirror to the viewer in order to affect change for the unfortunate people to whom this has happened.

I first reached out to several exonerees in the Western Pennsylvania area and got no response. But I wasn't going to let the project die. After a month went by I began to research the Innocence Project, affiliated with the Benjamin N. Cardozo School of Law at Yeshiva University, and similar organizations across the country, and came across an advertisement for a play called "Voices of Innocence." The play was written by four death row exonerees in New Orleans, Louisiana. I figured that

Dan Bolick in front of his Michael Graham (left) and Albert Burrell (right) paintings

if they had already turned their horrible experiences into art, they would be more open to my project. I was right. They agreed to allow me to come down to New Orleans to meet with them.

In May 2008, on that first trip to New Orleans, I met John Thompson. John, who spent eighteen years incarcerated for a murder he did not commit—fourteen of those on death row—is one of the authors of the play. He is the founder of Resurrection After Exoneration, which provides support for the wrongfully convicted after they are released from prison. The organization has built an incredibly inspiring and cooperative community.

Imagine what it's like to lose decades of your life and not be compensated for your loss.

I showed John some photos of my portraits and explained my project to him. He was enthusiastic about it from the beginning and began to contact other exonerees who would allow me to do their portraits. I could not have gotten this project off the ground without the help of John. John's wrongful death sentence and death row incarceration is the subject of a new book titled "Killing Time."

Imagine, if you can, what it must feel like to have the state take your life. Now imagine what it must feel like knowing that you are INNOCENT of the crime that you have been condemned for doing! To me it is unimaginable and incomprehensible, but to the human beings depicted in "Resurrected," it was their daily reality. When an innocent person is released from long term incarceration, imagine what it's like to be welcomed back by a society that is not waiting with open arms. Imagine what it's like to never receive an official apology for the wrong that was done to you. For the majority of the folks that I have painted there has been a great reluctance by the state to even acknowledge that a mistake had been made. Imagine what it's like to not be eligible for services to help re-enter society, such as psychological counseling, job training, education, and housing assistance—services meant for GUILTY offenders only—not the wrongfully convicted. Imagine what it's like to lose decades of your life and not be compensated for your loss.

I would eventually paint the portraits of thirteen people who suffered the unimaginable injustice of wrongful conviction. These thirteen truly inspirational people depicted in my paintings and drawings have experienced some of the most excruciatingly torturous situations ever faced by man. They have served 203 years in prison—71 on death row—for crimes THEY DID NOT COMMIT!

I call my exhibit "Resurrected." Since June of 2009, "Resurrected" has been exhibited at The Westmoreland Museum of American Art in Greensburg, Pennsylvania; Penn State University; Point Park University in Pittsburgh, Pennsylvania; Westmoreland Community College in Youngwood, Pennsylvania; and at South Texas College in McAllen, Texas. After my exhibit leaves the National Underground Freedom Center, The Westmoreland Museum is planning to "tour" the show, hopefully to a wider audience.

I hope that "Resurrected" will raise awareness about the failings of the criminal justice system. Art can engage a person when they don't expect it. People, in general, don't want to be reminded of the failings of our society. Everyone knows it's there, but "it's someone else's problem." I don't want the viewer to be able to escape the gaze of the people in these paintings and drawings when they walk into the National Underground Freedom Center. I want the viewer to see anger, bitterness, hope, acceptance, and salvation and ultimate resurrection. What happened to these unfortunate people is intolerable. Wrongful convictions happen everyday. It should not be accepted.

DAN **BRIGHT**

SERVED 10 YEARS OF A DEATH SENTENCE

NEW ORLEANS, LOUISIANA

Dan spent ten years at Angola State Prison in Louisiana for a murder and robbery he did not commit. Dan was convicted in 1996. The crime took place outside a bar in the Ninth Ward in New Orleans.

Dan's trial lawyer completed no investigation of the case and was drunk during the trial, thus, making a poor job of his defense. Dan's trial lasted two days and ended with a death sentence.

It later emerged that the F.B.I. had been in possession of the name of the real killer all along. Despite requests made by the Freedom of Information Act that the information be released, the U.S. government took the perspective that the killer's privacy rights were implicated, declining to reveal the name. It took a lawsuit in federal district court to resolve the impasse, with the judge finding that Dan had the right to the information. The identity of the real killer, together with other evidence, was presented in the state district court and eventually the Supreme Court of Louisiana reversed Dan's conviction.

Dan was released, much to the relief of not just his family, but also of Kathleen Hawk Norman, the jury foreperson that had convicted Dan and who later campaigned for his exoneration. Kathleen became the board chairperson for The Innocence Project of New Orleans.

Dan's case is illustrative of the issues of government accountability and how wrongful conviction cases need reform so that the priorities are aimed at protecting the innocent.

Dan is now rebuilding his life and works as a mentor to at-risk youth in inner city New Orleans.

BOLICK

GREG **BRIGHT**

SERVED 27.5 YEARS OF A LIFE SENTENCE

NEW ORLEANS, LOUISIANA

Greg spent twenty-seven-and-a-half years in the Louisiana State Prison System for a crime he did not commit. Greg was convicted in 1975 of second degree murder and sentenced to life in prison without parole. At the time Greg was twenty years old.

Greg's conviction was based solely on the testimony of a single supposed eyewitness. The jury never heard from the Coroner, who would have testified that the time of death did not coincide with the time that the witness claimed that she saw the murder. Nor did the jury know that the eyewitness was a paranoid schizophrenic who suffered from auditory and visual hallucinations, who was medicating her mental illness with heroin, who gave the police information in exchange for cash, and was testifying under a false name to conceal her own problems with the law.

In 2002, Greg was granted a hearing at which The Innocence Project of New Orleans demonstrated not only the problems with the single eyewitness, but also that the State had concealed a police report describing alternate suspects. Greg's conviction was overturned and he was granted a new trial. On June 24th, 2003, after twenty-seven-and-a-half years, Greg was released after the Orleans Parish District Attorney dropped all charges. He left prison with nothing but a ten dollar check from the State of Louisiana, and a garbage bag full of legal paperwork.

Greg is now rebuilding his life. He and three other exonerates have created a series of monologues detailing their experiences called, "Voices of Innocence." So far, "Voices of Innocence" has been performed at Harvard University, Tulane University and at the University of Illinois College of Law.

BOLICK 08

ALBERT **BURRELL**

SERVED 14 YEARS OF A DEATH SENTENCE

UNION PARISH, LOUISIANA

Albert spent fourteen years on death row at Angola State Prison in Louisiana for a crime he did not commit. He was convicted of the same crime as Michael Graham: the brutal murder of an elderly couple in northern Louisiana. Albert, who is mentally challenged and unable to read or write, came within seventeen days of execution in 1996.

Albert's case is an example of serious prosecutorial misconduct. With no physical evidence linking him to the crime, he was convicted largely on the testimony of a jail house snitch, Olan Wayne Brantley, who a law enforcement official acknowledged as, "Lyin' Wayne." Mr. Brantley said that Albert, while in jail, had confessed to killing the elderly couple. Mr. Brantley admitted at his trial that he had spent time in several mental hospitals and that he had written so many bad checks that he could not keep track of them. The prosecution did not disclose that a plea bargain had been made with Mr. Brantley, or that Mr. Brantley had previously been found to be mentally incompetent.

No witness put Albert at the scene of the killing, nor did the ballistic tests of his guns link him to the deaths.

The kind of prosecutorial misconduct present in Albert's case is not unusual. It is a problem that is inherent in the criminal justice system.

Upon his release from prison, Albert, like Michael Graham, was issued a denim jacket several sizes too large and a ten dollar check for transportation.

BOLICK

CLYDE **CHARLES**

SERVED 18 YEARS OF A LIFE SENTENCE

HOUMA, LOUISIANA

Clyde spent eighteen years in Louisiana's State Penitentiary at Angola for a crime he did not commit. Clyde was found guilty of aggravated rape on June 22nd, 1982. He was sentenced to life in prison.

Clyde appealed his case twice, in 1982 and in 1987, and lost both times. Then, in 1990, he learned about DNA evidence. He and his sisters began writing letters requesting a test of the evidence in his case. For years their requests were ignored by state and federal officials. Eventually, The Innocence Project took his case.

The State of Louisiana, under pressure from The Innocence Project and from media attention from the "Frontline" television series, finally granted Clyde DNA testing in May of 1999 and he was released on December 17th, 1999.

Four months later, his brother Marlo was arrested after DNA tests implicated him in the rape (Marlo is now in Angola).

After his release, Clyde lived in and out of his car on the bayou in Houma, Louisiana. He suffered from severe bouts of depression and diabetes, which went untreated.

Sadly, Clyde passed away January 9th, 2009. At last he found true freedom.

BOLICK

CLARENCE **ELKINS**

SERVED 7.5 YEARS OF A LIFE SENTENCE

SUMMIT COUNTY, OHIO

Full story in Part II, page 88

BOLICK

MICHAEL **GRAHAM**

SERVED 14 YEARS OF A DEATH SENTENCE

UNION PARISH, LOUISIANA

Michael Graham spent fourteen years on death row at the Louisiana State Prison at Angola for a crime he did not commit. Represented at trial by two inexperienced attorneys, one of whom abandoned the case before the sentencing phase, Michael was convicted of the murder of an elderly couple in 1987.

During his years on death row, Michael spent twenty-three hours a day in a 5 x 10 foot cell, alone. He was allowed out one hour a day to shower and walk up and down the jail tier. Three times a week he could go outside and spend an hour by himself in the exercise yard. Whenever he left his tier, his hands and legs were shackled. Everyone in his world was either a prison guard, who considered him an animal, or a condemned man. The guards told him when to wake up and when to go to sleep, and just gave him a few minutes to eat.

The case against Michael consisted of three witnesses, who later recanted their testimony, and a prosecution that withheld evidence of his innocence. In March of 2000, with the help of pro-bono lawyers, Michael won a new trial. He was freed from prison nine months later on December 28th. After fourteen years of wrongful imprisonment, the state of Louisiana gave Michael a ten dollar check and an overcoat that was five sizes too big. At the time of his release, Michael had spent half of his adult life on death row.

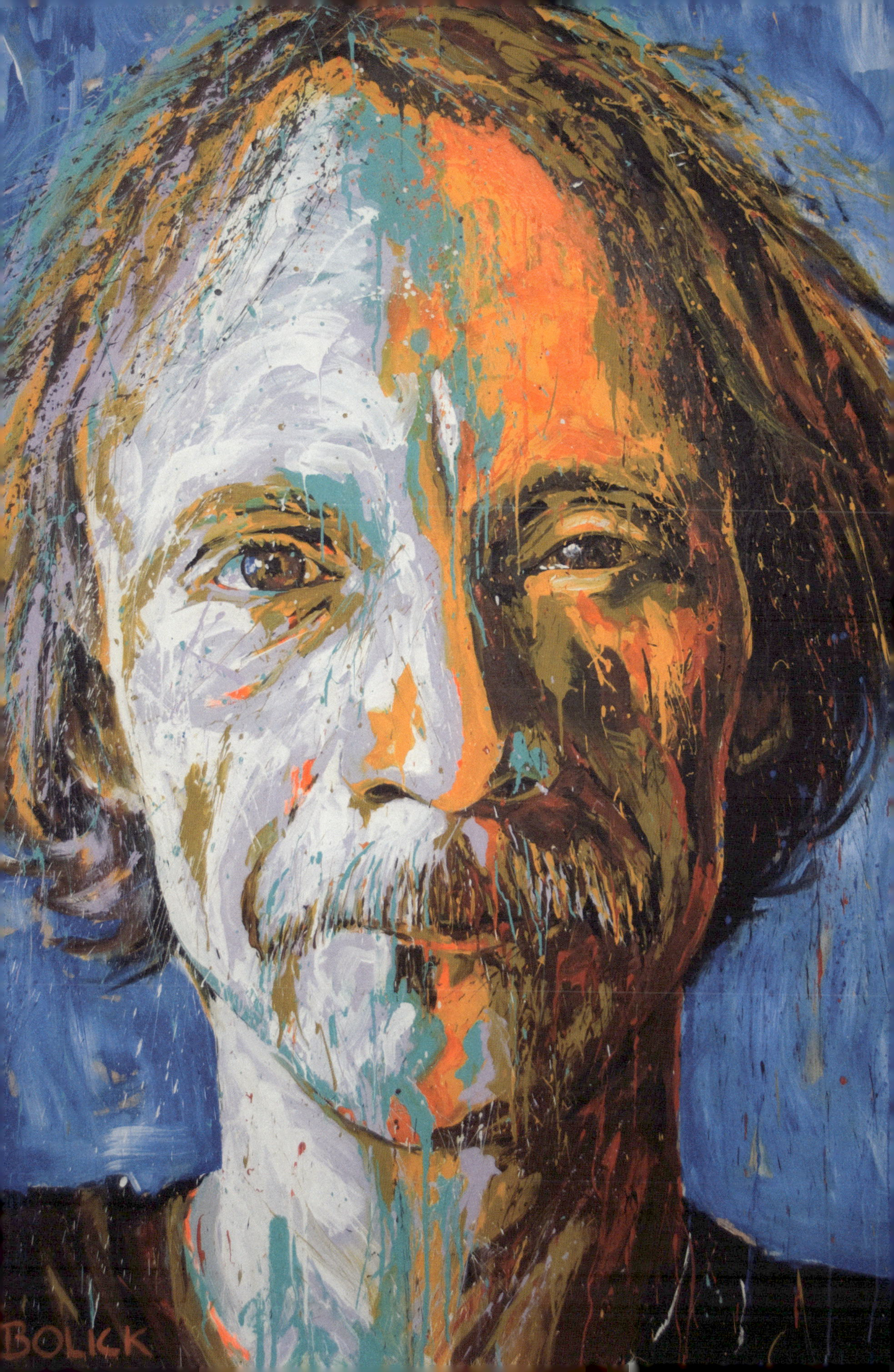
BOLICK

CURTIS **KYLES**

SERVED 18 YEARS OF A DEATH SENTENCE

NEW ORLEANS, LOUISIANA

Curtis spent eighteen years in the Louisiana State Penitentiary at Angola, fourteen years on death row, for a murder he did not commit. Curtis was tried five times for the same crime. At one point, he came within thirty hours of execution.

Curtis was arrested in 1984 for the murder of Delores Dye, a sixty-year-old housewife and mother, during a car theft in a grocery store parking lot. His first trial ended in a hung jury. A month later, he was retried, convicted, and sentenced to death.

During the appeals process, eyewitnesses recanted their stories and it was discovered that the State prosecutors had withheld critical information about another witness: a paid police informant who might have been the actual killer. This informant also profited from a reward that had been offered in the case by the victim's family.

Having lost all of his appeals in state courts as well as the U.S. Fifth Circuit Court of Appeals, Curtis' case was accepted to be heard by The United States Supreme Court. In a decision that was given just a few days before he was to be executed, the Supreme Court ruled Curtis was entitled to a new trial because there was, "reasonable probability" that the disclosure of the state-concealed evidence would have produced a different result in the trial.

However, Curtis' journey through the criminal justice system was far from over. His third trial, in October 1996, ended in a deadlocked jury and subsequent trials in the next two years had the same result. After the fourth and fifth trials ended in hung juries, prosecutors decided to drop the charges. Curtis was released but was never officially declared innocent. Curtis' case was one of the most thoroughly adjudicated in history.

CRY.
BOLICK

RYAN **MATTHEWS**

SERVED 5 YEARS OF A DEATH SENTENCE

BRIDGE CITY, LOUISIANA

Ryan spent five years on death row at the Louisiana State Prison at Angola for a crime he did not commit. Seventeen years old at the time of arrest, Ryan was sentenced to death for the shooting death of a convenience store owner.

In April 1997, a man wearing a ski mask entered a convenience store in Bridge City, Louisiana and demanded money. When the owner, Tommy Vanhoose, refused, the perpetrator shot him four times and fled, diving into the passenger side window of a getaway car.

Two witnesses in another car watched as the perpetrator shed his mask, gloves and shirt. The driver claimed to have seen the perpetrator's face in his rearview mirror as he was being shot at for trying to block the perpetrator's escape. Hours later, the witness identified Ryan in a line-up. The passenger was unable to make an identification.

Because his car resembled the description of the getaway car, Ryan was stopped and arrested several hours after the crime. Police questioned him for over six hours. They described him as being borderline mentally retarded.

At trial, Ryan's defense presented evidence of forensic testing of the mask that excluded Ryan. A defense expert also testified that the car Ryan was driving could not be the getaway car because the passenger side window could not be rolled down. Other witnesses to the crime described the shooter as being much shorter than Ryan. Regardless, in 1999, Ryan was convicted of murder and sentenced to death.

Continued defense investigation discovered Rondell Love, a local resident, was arrested and pled guilty to another murder in the same area as Vanhoose's. Love bragged to other inmates that he also killed Vanhoose. DNA test results from the second murder proved that Love had been wearing the mask that was left behind in the Vanhoose murder.

Over a year after this information was discovered, Ryan was granted a new trial. He was released in June 2004 on bond as he awaited a new trial. In August 2004, prosecutors asked the court to lift the bond and vacate Ryan's conviction. He was a free man.

Ryan was the fourteenth death row inmate in the United States to be proven innocent by post-conviction DNA testing.

BOLICK

ROBERT **MCCLENDON**

SERVED 17 YEARS OF A LIFE SENTENCE

COLUMBUS, OHIO

Full story in Part II, page 142

BOLICK

NANCY **SMITH**

SERVED 14.5 YEARS OF A 90 YEAR SENTENCE

LORAIN, OHIO

Full story in Part II, page 180

BOLICK

JOHN THOMPSON

SERVED 18 YEARS OF A DEATH SENTENCE

NEW ORLEANS, LOUISIANA

John spent eighteen years in Angola State Prison in Louisiana, fourteen of those years on death row, for a murder he did not commit.

In 1995, after John had spent eleven years on death row, the lead prosecutor at John's trial, Jerry Deagen, made a stunning disclosure. He told fellow prosecutor Mike Riehlmann he was dying of liver cancer and had a confession: he had concealed blood evidence that could prove John's innocence.

Incredibly, after Deagen died, Riehlmann said nothing of his friend's confession for five years while John sat in a cell waiting for his date with the electric chair.

Riehlmann eventually went public with Deagen's confession in 1999 and was briefly suspended by the Louisiana Supreme Court for his inaction.

John spent fourteen of eighteen years in Angola on death row and survived seven execution dates.

Like other exonerees from Louisiana, John left Angola with a small bag of possessions and ten dollars for bus fare.

John's life after exoneration is truly inspirational. "Echoing Green," a New York based foundation that supports social entrepreneurs, invested more in John than Louisiana did. He received a two-year $60,000 grant to establish "Resurrection After Exoneration," an organization designed to give wrongfully convicted victims the financial, emotional and vocational skills needed to live a successful post-prison life.

BOLICK

DREW **WHITLEY**

SERVED 18 YEARS OF A LIFE SENTENCE

DUQUESNE, PENNSYLVANIA

Drew spent eighteen years in the Pennsylvania State Correctional Institution for a crime he did not commit. He was sentenced to life imprisonment for second degree murder in the 1988 shooting death of Noreen Malloy at a McDonald's restaurant near Kennywood Park.

The perpetrator, who wore a trench coat, stocking mask and a felt hat, could not be identified by any of the witnesses. Police eventually found a witness who said that he looked directly at the assailant from a distance of three feet but did not know who he was. After twenty-six hours of repeated interrogations, the witness named Drew as the killer.

The witness's story contradicted so much of the collected evidence that police did not immediately file charges against Drew. Hair and fingerprints collected at the scene did not match Drew's and DNA testing was unavailable at the time. However, Drew was jailed the next day on a technical parole violation.

Six months later, Gary Starr, a double murderer on death row said that while in prison Drew had confessed to the Malloy killing even though Starr was isolated on death row and would not have had access to Drew in prison. Within a year of Drew's trial, Starr's death sentence was reduced to life in prison.

After DNA testing came into widespread use in the 90s, Drew fought for six years to be granted DNA testing. Police officials said they lost all but two of the hairs collected at the crime scene during a flood at Police headquarters. In 2003, police found the missing hair samples. In 2006, DNA profiling proved that the hair samples did not match Drew and he was exonerated.

Drew left prison with less than one hundred dollars from working in the prison laundry. Since his exoneration, Drew has not had much luck finding work, but is enjoying his freedom.

BOLICK

CALVIN **WILLIS**

SERVED 22 YEARS OF A LIFE SENTENCE

SHREVEPORT, LOUISIANA

Calvin served twenty-two years in Angola State Prison in Louisiana for a crime he did not commit. Calvin was convicted in February 1982 of the rape of a young girl and sentenced to life in prison without any possibility of parole.

From the time he was arrested Calvin denied having anything to do with the crime. Calvin's wife testified that they had spent the whole night together and that she was with him at the time of the crime.

The clothes he was wearing that night did not match those described by the victim or her two sisters who saw the perpetrator as he was leaving.

The girls knew Calvin from the neighborhood and testified that another man, who they did not know, wearing clothes similar to their description, had visited their home that night.

The jury did not believe any of Calvin's alibis.

In 1998 The Innocence Project accepted Calvin's case. Through their investigations they found long-missing physical evidence that was intentionally hidden in the clerk's office in the District Parish Court. DNA testing of this evidence excluded Calvin from being a contributor to any of the evidence samples.

On September 18th, 2003, Calvin was released from Angola and was greeted by his family. Calvin had spent twenty-two years in prison for a crime he did not commit.

BOLICK

PART II / EXPRESSIONS OF THE **WRONGFULLY CONVICTED**

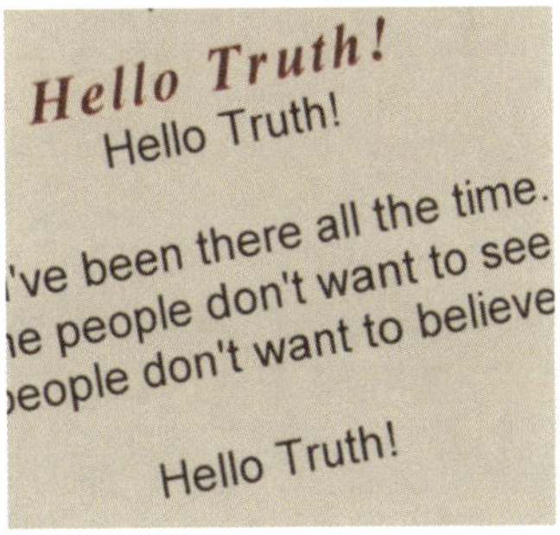

***The pain and frustration** of wrongful conviction and incarceration often manifests itself in incredibly meaningful forms of artistic expression. The wrongfully convicted have important things to say, and it is clear that art is a particularly powerful and effective way for them to say it.*

– Mark Godsey

STEVEN **BARNES**

SERVED 19.5 YEARS OF A 25 TO LIFE SENTENCE

PLACE OF TRIAL
UTICA, NEW YORK

Courtesy of the Innocence Project
Researched by Guy Cardamone, Claire Gutmann, and Jennifer Miller

On the evening of September 18, 1985, sixteen year old Kimberly Simon left her Marcy, New York, home to meet a friend. The next day police found her body near the side of the road. She had been raped and strangled to death.

Several people told police they had seen Simon walking along a busy street between 5:30 and 6:00 p.m. Others said they saw Steven Barnes' distinct truck on that road around the same time. Based on these vague statements from eyewitnesses, Barnes became a suspect.

Three days after the victim was last seen, Barnes was questioned for twelve hours straight. He told police that he had driven to a bowling alley at 6:00 p.m. on the night of the crime and did not know anything about the murder. He was given a polygraph test which investigators said was inconclusive. Police also checked his truck for Simon's fingerprints and trace evidence. He was released without charges. More than two years later, investigators still working the case asked Barnes to submit blood, saliva, and hair samples. He was subsequently arrested in March of 1988, more than two years after the crime, and charged with rape, sodomy, and murder.

Barnes was tried by a jury in Utica, New York, beginning on May 15, 1989. A forensic analyst testified at his trial that no fingerprints collected from Barnes' truck matched the victim's. Although tire print comparison has never been a validated forensic practice, the tracks from the crime scene were compared with Barnes' truck tires and investigators determined that they did not match.

Serological evidence was introduced at trial and also did not point to Barnes. Dr. Elaine Pagliaro, the supervising criminalist at the Connecticut State Police Forensic Laboratory, testified that seminal fluid was detected on the victim's underwear and on swabs taken from her body and that serology testing was conducted. The results matched the victim's blood type, but were inconclusive regarding Barnes, who is a non-secretor (his blood type is not revealed from bodily fluids such as semen and saliva). DNA testing conducted before trial was inconclusive.

Three forms of unvalidated forensic science were used against Barnes at trial. Pagliaro testified that she conducted a photographic overlay of fabric from the victim's jeans and an imprint on Barnes' truck and determined that the two patterns were similar. The state then entered testimony from a self-employed manufacturer's representative who told the court that the stitching on the brand of jeans the victim wore was unique and that as many as 200 pairs may have been sold in Oneida County, New York, in 1985.

Barnes' attorney called several witnesses who testified that Barnes was at a local bowling alley at the time the crime was allegedly committed.

Pagliaro also testified that two hairs collected from Barnes' truck were microscopically "similar" to the victim's hairs and dissimilar from Barnes' hair. She added that no hairs similar to Barnes' samples were found on the victim's body. Pagliaro's lab also compared soil samples taken from Steven's truck with dirt samples taken from the crime scene a year after the murder and testified that they had "similar characteristics." Microscopic hair analysis, soil comparison, and fabric print analysis have not been validated scientifically. Because there is not adequate empirical data on the frequency of various class characteristics in human hair, soil samples, or imprints, the analyst's assertion that these items of evidence were consistent or similar is inherently prejudicial and lacks probative value.

The state also introduced the testimony of a jailhouse informant, who said Barnes confessed to him while in jail awaiting trial more than two years after the crime. The informant, Robert Stolo, was in custody on forgery and larceny charges. He met Barnes at the jail and they were on the same cell block for about a week. Stolo told the court that he talked with Barnes along with another inmate, who had asked Barnes about some girls and Barnes purportedly asked in return, "You mean the one that I killed?" then corrected himself by saying, "I mean the one that I am accused of killing?" Stolo, however, was housed several cells away from Barnes and couldn't remember when or where this conversation happened. Stolo testified that he didn't expect a lighter sentence for his testimony, and that he received a one-year sentence for his conviction.

Barnes' attorney called several witnesses who testified that Barnes was at a local bowling alley at the time the crime was allegedly committed. He was convicted of rape and murder and sentenced to twenty-five years to life in prison.

The Innocence Project, a national litigation and public policy organization dedicated to exonerating the wrongfully convicted through DNA testing, began representing Barnes in 1993 and repeatedly secured DNA testing for him. However, all tests were inconclusive until 2007 when advanced Y-STR DNA testing became available. The new tests conclusively established sperm cells from the victim's body and clothing did not match Barnes.

After serving almost two decades in prison for a murder and rape he didn't commit, Barnes was freed on November 25, 2008. His exoneration became official on January 9, 2009, when prosecutors announced that they were dropping all charges against him. Shortly after his exoneration he celebrated his forty-third birthday—the first one as a free man in two decades.

"Covered Bridge" / STEVEN BARNES

I painted this in prison wishing that one day I would be a free man again and could walk through a bridge like this.

"Deer" / *STEVEN BARNES*

This was painted in prison hoping that someday soon I would see this scene for myself and be free to explore nature again.

LEVON BROOKS

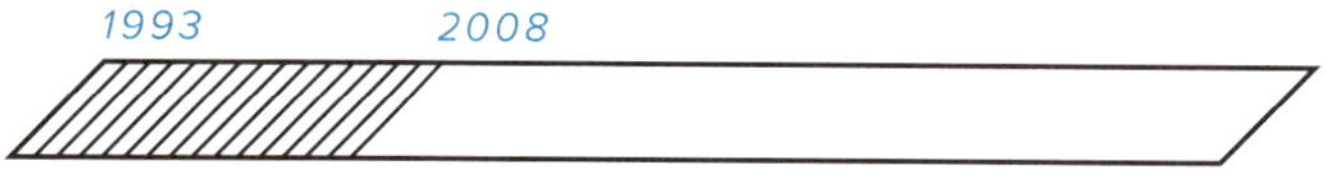

SERVED 16 YEARS OF A LIFE SENTENCE

PLACE OF TRIAL
NOXUBEE COUNTY, MISSISSIPPI

Written by Clement Tsao
Researched by Andrew Cleves and Sean Martz

In 1990, three year old Courtney Smith was abducted from her home in the middle of the night. She was raped and murdered and her body was later found in a pond near her home in Noxubee County, Mississippi. Levon Brooks was dating Smith's mother at the time of the crime. Prosecutors focused their attention on him even though the man who later turned out to be the true perpetrator, Justin Johnson, was also an initial suspect during the investigation.

Brooks' conviction was based mostly on the false forensic testimony of dentist Dr. Michael West and uncertified state pathologist, Dr. Steven Hayne, who conducted Smith's autopsy. After Hayne identified bite-marks on the body, West testified that he could definitively match the marks to Brooks. Johnson had been excluded from further investigation because of this bite-mark comparison. Brooks was convicted of the rape and murder of Smith and was sentenced to life in prison without parole.

The Innocence Project, a national litigation and public policy organization dedicated to exonerating the wrongfully convicted through DNA testing, began representing Kennedy Brewer, another man who had been convicted of a similar crime with the use of the same false forensic testimony used against Brooks. DNA testing in Brewer's case implicated Johnson who later confessed to the raping and killing of both children. The DNA testing, combined with Johnson's confession, led to the release and exoneration of both Brewer and Brooks – and raised serious questions about the way forensic science was performed in Mississippi.

According to the Innocence Project, the forensic analysis and testimony in both trials were deeply flawed thus illustrating the level of corruption that led to the wrongful convictions of Brooks and Brewer. Both men's cases were investigated by the same sheriff's deputy and prosecuted by the same District Attorney. Hayne conducted nearly every autopsy for the state of Mississippi even though he failed his board certification exam. According to the Innocence Project, it was also well known in Mississippi that Hayne and West tailored their findings to suit the needs of prosecutors in their prosecutions. It was this conduct that sent Brooks to prison for life and Brewer to death row. Several findings made by Hayne and West have recently been overturned in court because they were found not to have been based on credible science or fact. In order to ensure justice for its clients, the Innocence Project convinced the Mississippi State Attorney General's Office to intervene and take the case from local prosecutors upon the confession of Johnson.

The DNA testing...raised serious questions about the way forensic science was performed in Mississippi.

On March 13, 2008, after serving fifteen years in prison, Brooks was fully exonerated and walked out of the courtroom a free man. Citing the Brewer and Brooks cases, the Mississippi legislature passed legislation to create a task force on handling DNA evidence and in 2009 Governor Haley Barbour signed a DNA preservation bill into law. Prior to the signing of this bill, Mississippi was one of eight states that did not have a law granting post-conviction DNA testing.

"Bird Drawing" / LEVON BROOKS

When I was in prison, I designed cards for people. They could be anniversary cards or celebration cards or different stuff like that. This was one of my leading sellers. I was inspired by people's relationships and how important they are.

DARRYL **BURTON**

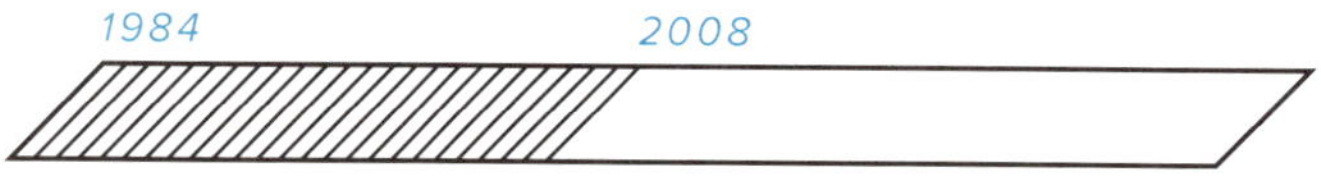

SERVED 24 YEARS OF A LIFE SENTENCE

PLACE OF TRIAL
ST. LOUIS, MISSOURI

Written by Lourdes Perrino
Researched by Zach El-Sawaf and Dominique Mix

On June, 4, 1984, well-known crack-cocaine dealer Donald "Moe" Ball was shot and killed while pumping gas at a station in St. Louis, Missouri. Ball had been involved in an on-going turf war with a rival dealer, Jesse Watson. Watson had previously shot Ball in the same neighborhood, but had failed to kill him. One month after the murder, twenty-two year old Darryl Burton was arrested by St. Louis police officers for the murder of Ball.

The officers based the arrest on information they had obtained from a street informant and a prison snitch. At Burton's two-day trial in March of 1985, the witnesses testified that they had been near the gas station the night of the murder and had seen Burton shoot Ball. Both witnesses had made deals with the prosecutor for lesser sentences in unrelated crimes in exchange for their testimony implicating Burton as the gunman.

There was no physical evidence connecting Burton to the crime. Other witnesses' reports identifying the gunman as lighter-skinned and shorter in height than Burton was not presented to the jury. Some witnesses even identified Watson as the gunman that night, but he was never investigated by police nor was his prior shooting of Ball presented to the jury. Regardless of the lack of evidence and after less than an hour of deliberation, the jury convicted Burton of capital murder and he was sentenced to life in prison. Upon leaving the courtroom, Burton told the judge that someday he would prove the court condemned the wrong man.

Despite his consuming anger at the injustice done to him, Burton spent his time in prison determined to prove his innocence. After exhausting traditional state court remedies, Burton's hope of exonerating himself was renewed when he received an affidavit from the prison snitch who had testified against him at his trial. In the affidavit, the snitch admitted he had perjured his testimony. With this new information, Burton began reaching out to nonprofit organizations, congressmen, and other government leaders who might help him find a way to prove his innocence.

With his 600 plus letters having gone unanswered, Burton wrote the letter that changed his life; he wrote to God. Burton had never been much of a believer and his jury conviction had further ingrained his lack of faith. With nothing else to lose, Burton decided to take a chance. He wrote, "If you're real, then you know, like I know, that I'm innocent. So if you help me get out of this place, not only will I serve you, but I will tell the world about you."

In 2000, Burton received a letter from Centurion Ministries, an organization that works to free the convicted innocent throughout the United States and Canada. On May 16, 2002, the Centurion Ministries lawyers who had taken Burton's case filed a habeas corpus petition with the United States Court of Appeals for the Eighth Circuit arguing that Burton's constitutional rights had been violated during trial. The court did not agree and denied the petition. The United States Supreme Court foreclosed Burton's last hope of exoneration when it denied his request for review of the circuit court's decision.

On April 29, 2003, the day after the Supreme Court made its decision, the Missouri Supreme Court exonerated an innocent man on death row based on new DNA evidence proving the man's innocence. Implicit in its decision was the Missouri Supreme Court's willingness to review claims of innocence based on new evidence—giving Burton his last chance of being exonerated. Burton's attorneys immediately seized the opportunity and began investigating the twenty-five year old crime. Through the discovery process, Burton's attorneys found out that Watson, the real gunman, had admitted to friends that he murdered Ball after Burton was already convicted of the crime.

In the affidavit, the snitch admitted he had perjured his testimony.

Armed with this new evidence, Burton's attorneys were able to eventually present their case to the U.S. Court of Appeals for the Eighth Circuit where Judge Bye stated that although he believed Burton was innocent, his hands were procedurally tied. After this encouraging ruling, Burton's attorneys filed a state habeas corpus petition in the Missouri State Court where they were allowed to present all of the new evidence collected on Burton's case which eventually led to his exoneration. Having spent more than half his life in prison, on August 29, 2008, Burton walked out of the Jefferson City Correction Center a free man.

Today Burton lives in Kansas City where he works as a life coach to young children. He is also a motivational speaker traveling around the United States to share his story and working to help free other wrongly convicted prisoners. Burton has also recently filed a lawsuit in federal court against the City of St. Louis, the Mayor, the St. Louis Board of Police Commissioners, and several police officers alleging the police suppressed eyewitness descriptions of the gunman, coached witnesses into accusing Burton of the murder, and created false police reports thus violating his constitutional rights.

"Crime & Consequence" / *DARRYL BURTON*

No one goes to prison in the United States of America for a crime they did not commit, I guarantee you this, that's a bunch of bull-shhh...

I was convicted of more than a high crime and misdemeanor, the conviction of capital murder is like espionage or treason...

I was convicted of one of the big three, not for espionage or treason, but I was wrongfully convicted of capital murder and the state never gave me a reason...

The family of the victim lost their loved one on a gas station lot, and the police had to solve this crime and so they began to plot...

The police didn't have a motive, a weapon, DNA evidence, a fingerprint, or a confession connecting me to this crime, so you'd think that would make them stop, but no they arrested me anyway and said for the rest of my days in prison, I would rot...

Justice can never be served when there is a rush to lock up the innocent and throw away the key, and it is true that injustice is not blind and she really can see...

When the police and prosecutors manipulated the criminal justice system and railroaded me, they deliberately wrapped a picture frame around me that Ray Charles could see...

This happened in a black community, and it was a so-called black-on-black crime, and so a black man was going to pay for this charge and do a whole lot of time...

I have to say that this crime and punishment created many victims all along the line, on both sides of the entire situation...

Everyone lost loved ones in this whole criminal process which was a tragic demonstration of human suffering and total humiliation...

My daughter was seven months old when I last saw her and the state being determined to send me away to prison for a crime I did not commit...

We were separated for 24 years for this wrongful sentence that created two prisons and no one can offer an explanation for this...

There were nights I would dream of her asking the questions, mommy where's my daddy at, and why has he left us all alone...?

A reply that dropped a tear from my eye, was daddy loves you baby and he is a way for awhile, but some day he will come home...

Who will deny the fact that people who seek to solve crimes create crimes themselves, and for all crimes there is a legal, spiritual or moral consequence...

And for those who can never repay me for the 24 years of false imprisonment, for all the time I lost with my daughter, my family and community, it is these kinds of crimes and the unpunished that keep society stooped in ignorance and cloaked in suspense...

This poem was written to express the loss and frustration I had to endure from being separated from my child and loved ones. It is also to reflect the fact that those who are in power commit crimes against citizens of this country and nothing is done to them because of their "qualified immunity." I have to say that there is no date for this compilation because the pain and agony of it all is just as real today as it was the first day I was arrested wrongfully and sent to prison when it was clear that they had the wrong man.

"Human Nature" / DARRYL BURTON

Human nature is a very strange animal...
Sometimes it is meek and mild, carefree and wild...

Vicious and suspicious, ironically very religious...
Mean and serene, a calm, yet turbulent machine...

Love and hate, forgiveness and mistakes...
A verbal expression of affection, a call that is innate in us all...

A silent emotion, the roaring billows of an ocean...
Human nature is the lion's desire, the passion before the fire...

It is disruption and confusion, aberrations and illusions...
It is a rollercoaster of change, yet aspiring and inspiration remains...

It is anxiety and depression, development and correction...
The sensation of procreation, loneliness and preoccupation...

Revolution for liberation, rebellion sit-downs and demonstrations...
Sad hearts and wrecked minds, healed wounds and better times...

It is behavioral mystiques, let-downs and disbeliefs...
Ethnicities and multicultural, notwithstanding, all of whom are vulnerable...

Prejudice and perceptions, humble, wholesome and perfectionist...
Active and aggressive, tranquil, calm and a pacifist...

Attractive and unique, futuristic and obsolete...
It is many tests that pass as casual, a human quest that is all so natural...

The poem is an expression of Human Nature and how people do all these things for causes and conditions that may or may not bring just results. But the theme is to simply say human beings do human things right, wrong or indifferent. It may not be what you want but it is something that describes all of us in one form or another. Even those who represented bad lawyer ethics in these innocence cases.

KEITH **BUSH**

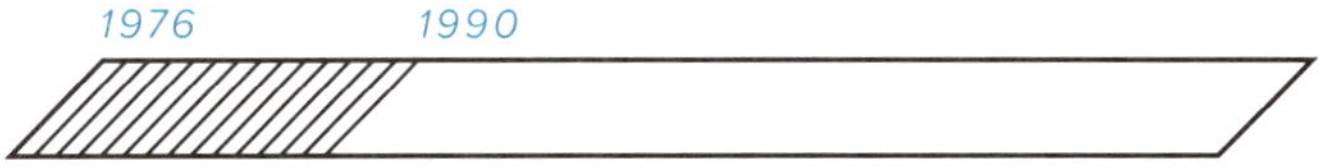

SERVED 14 YEARS OF A 30 TO 90 YEAR SENTENCE

PLACE OF TRIAL

LONG ISLAND, NEW YORK

Courtesy of Adele Bernhard, Pace Law School Post-Conviction Project
Researched by Megan Collard and Lindsey Fleissner

In January, 1975, the body of fourteen year old Sharese Watson was found in a field near a home in Suffolk County, Long Island, where scores of young people had partied two nights earlier. Watson had been strangled to death. There were so many people at the party no one could say exactly when Watson left, nor were there any clues as to the identity of her killer.

Party-goer, seventeen year old Keith Bush, was asked to go to the police station in order to identify other people at the party. Upon arrival at the police station, he was read his Miranda rights and was arrested for Watson's murder. After his arrest, Bush was interrogated and physically threatened by police until he confessed that he had stabbed Watson with a comb and then strangled her to death when she resisted his sexual advances. Focusing exclusively on Bush, police ignored other likely suspects, such as the older boys who had arrived at the party in a stolen car and who have since accumulated criminal records for murder, rape, and incest.

The evidence presented at trial consisted of Bush's signed "confession" which he immediately repudiated; a metal afro-pick style comb turned over to the police by Bush's brother, which was never linked to the crime by forensic evidence; fiber evidence linking Bush's jacket to the victim; and the testimony of several teens who attended the party. The most significant prosecution witness was a girl who was fifteen years old at the time of the murder who later recanted her testimony while under oath at a post-conviction hearing.

At trial, the prosecutor argued that Watson desperately fought and struggled with her attacker before succumbing to the attack. When the police discovered her body, the crime scene unit bagged her hands to protect whatever trace evidence might have been defensively scratched from the body of her assailant. At autopsy, the bags were removed and the forensic pathologist scraped beneath the victim's finger nails in the hope of finding skin or blood from her attacker. A police technician testified that there was no biological material under the victim's fingernails, but that cloth fiber found under her fingernails "matched" fibers in Bush's jacket. On June 16, 1976, Bush was convicted of second degree murder and attempted sexual abuse in the first degree. He was sentenced to thirty to ninety years imprisonment.

Thirty years later, advanced DNA technology identified human tissue, foreign to the victim in the scrapings, proving the technician wrong. The DNA testing definitively excluded Bush as the source of the male tissue found beneath the victim's fingernails, thus providing compelling proof that someone other than Bush attacked and killed Watson.

After his arrest, Bush was interrogated and physically threatened by police until he confessed...

The discovery of DNA evidence proving Bush's innocence should be sufficient to vacate his conviction, but so far Adele Bernhard and the Pace Law School Post-Conviction Project have not convinced the trial court of that. They are continuing to test crime scene evidence in the hopes of identifying a complete DNA profile. If a complete profile is identified, it could be entered into the FBI supported database, CODIS, which contains a DNA profile for all previously convicted felons. By entering the unidentified profile into this database a match could be discovered that would reveal the real perpetrator of this crime. They are also investigating alternative suspects.

Keith Bush is currently out on parole, living with his mother, and working steadily since his release. He also passed a polygraph test as required by the Department of Parole, further demonstrating his innocence of the crimes for which he was convicted in 1975.

"The Criminal Injustice System" / *KEITH BUSH*

THIRTY-TWO-PLUS YEARS OF FALSE IMPRISONMENT HAVE PIERCED
MY SOUL. CONSISTENT DENIALS TURNED ME FROM YOUNG TO OLD
AND YOU WONDER, WHY? WHY DOES HE ACT SO COLD? COULD
IT BE BECAUSE MY EXPERIENCE HAS TAUGHT ME,
NOTHING HAS CHANGED! THE PLANTATION AND
PRISON SYSTEM ARE ONE AND THE SAME

FUCK YOUR CRIMINAL INJUSTICE SYSTEM!

AND ALL YOU FAKE-ASS PATRIOTS, PRETENDING
TO REPRESENT JUSTICE IN THE NAME OF
DEMOCRACY, OR SHOULD I SAY, IN
THIS STOLEN LAND WHERE ONLY THE
RICH AND LIKED RECEIVE EQUALITY

SIT YOUR ASS DOWN MRS. LIBERTY

I AM SICK AND TIRED OF YOUR FUCKIN' HYPOCRISY
STANDING FOR JUSTICE IN DISGUISE
PRETENDING TO LOVE US ALL
ARE NOTHING BUT LIES

I KNOW YOU CAN SEE, SO TAKE THAT TRANSPARENT
CLOTH FROM AROUND YOUR EYES

HOW IN THE HELL CAN YOU BE BLIND:

WHEN IT COMES TO OPPRESSION AND INCARCERATION
THE POOR ARE THE ONLY ONES YOU CAN FIND

WHEN IT COMES TO CREATING AND ENFORCING LAWS
YOU DO SO TO PROTECT YOUR OWN WEALTHY KIND

AND YOU REALLY EXPECT ME TO
BELIEVE NONE OF THIS IS BY DESIGN

THAT'S RIGHT! YOU HEARD WHAT I SAID:

FUCK YOUR CRIMINAL INJUSTICE SYSTEM!

AND IF YOU DON'T LIKE THIS POEM THEN,

FUCK YOU TOO!!!

AL CLEVELAND

CURRENTLY SERVING 14 YEARS OF A LIFE SENTENCE

PLACE OF CRIME
LORAIN, OHIO

Written and Researched by Hilly McGahan
Researched by Lauren Creditt

On the morning of August 8, 1991, the bodies of twenty-two year old Marsha Blakely and Floyd Epps were found within a quarter mile of each other in Lorain, Ohio. They had both been murdered and run over by a car. Blakely had been stabbed twenty-five times.

A month after the murders, the Lorain Police Department had yet to solve the murders. When the Prosecutor's Office offered a $2,000 reward, William Avery Jr., a twenty-three year old local crack addict, came forward to tell police he had witnessed Blakely's murder. Avery Jr.'s uncorroborated eyewitness testimony led to the convictions of four men, including twenty-one year old Al Cleveland from Jamaica Queens, New York.

In his trial testimony, Avery Jr. claimed he owed Cleveland a drug debt he was unable to pay but Cleveland offered to forgive the debt if Avery Jr. would assault Blakely, another indebted addict. Avery Jr. claimed he refused Cleveland's offer because he knew Blakely and did not want to harm her. He further testified that Cleveland and Avery Jr. then stood by while Cleveland's friends beat Blakely for twenty minutes, forcibly removed her from her apartment, and murdered her behind a local bar. Avery Jr.'s testimony did not account for the murder of Epps.

The only evidence linking Cleveland and his friends to Blakely's murder was the uncorroborated eyewitness testimony of Avery Jr. Although the prosecution conceded that Cleveland had met with his probation officer in New York on the day that Blakely was murdered in Ohio, Cleveland was convicted of aggravated murder and sentenced to life in prison.

Fifteen years after the murder, in 2006, Avery Jr. came forward to admit he had lied about witnessing Blakely's murder. In a sworn statement, Avery Jr. stated that he had given false testimony for the reward money he received and because prosecutors threatened him when he attempted to back out of his testimony during the first trial of Cleveland's codefendant.

Al Cleveland, now 41, has served fourteen years in prison for the murder of Marsha Blakely. Floyd Epps' murder remains unsolved.

Al (right) with Ohio exoneree Raymond Towler (left)

In 2008, Avery Jr. drove from Detroit to the Lorain County Court to recant his testimony that had resulted in Cleveland's conviction. However, once he took the stand at Cleveland's evidentiary hearing, Avery Jr. was warned that he would not receive immunity for his recantation. In fear that he would receive jail time for perjury in four previous trials, Avery Jr. exercised his Fifth Amendment right not to incriminate himself. As he left the courthouse, Avery Jr. told reporters, "Dude's innocent, but I don't feel I have to go to jail for thirty years" (*Cleveland*, at 13).

Al Cleveland, now forty-one, has served fourteen years in prison for the murder of Blakely. Epps' murder remains unsolved. The Ohio Innocence Project, a component of the Rosenthal Institute for Justice at the University of Cincinnati College of Law that assists the convicted innocent, represents Cleveland and has filed a habeas petition on his behalf based on his claims of actual innocence.

"Flood of Lies" / AL CLEVELAND

"Flood of Lies" / *AL CLEVELAND*

Front & Back

I don't have many words to describe this piece, but it represents the end of the artistic confines to which I have been bound for years, and marks the beginning of an inward journey of truth-telling in art and the expression of such by all means despite the look. No beauty right now, just a soul under pressure and an able hand in need, coming to grips with a few dreams it must let go. Upon further thought, this represents the feeling of many of us wrongfully incarcerated, serving Life sentences.

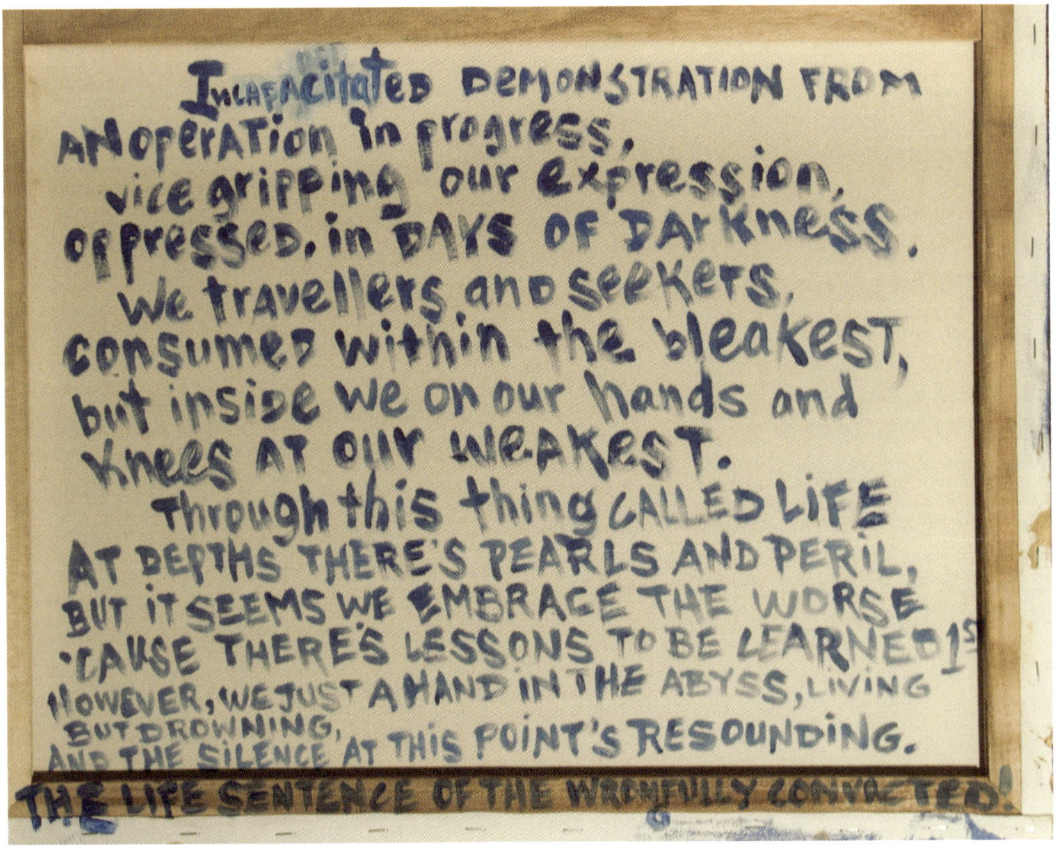

CHRIS CONOVER

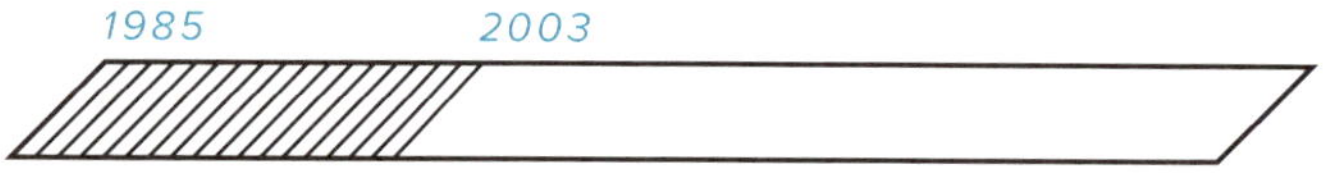

SERVED 18 YEARS OF A LIFE SENTENCE

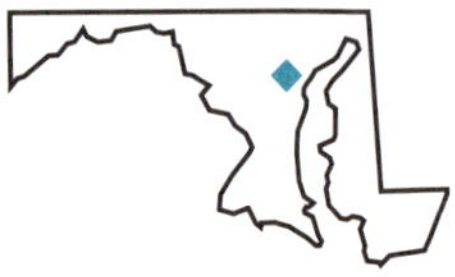

PLACE OF TRIAL
BALTIMORE, MARYLAND

Courtesy of the Mid-Atlantic Innocence Project
Researched by Patrick Bradley, Lauren Creditt, and Hilly McGahan

In the late hours of October 20, 1984, three men broke into the Baltimore, Maryland, home of noted drug dealer Charles "Squeaky" Jordan. Jordan, his wife Linda, and stepdaughter were all shot execution style. Linda survived the attack and described her assailants as two black men and a white man. She later identified African-American and fellow drug dealer, Gregory Jones, as the gunman in the murders. Because of his history of drug-related charges, and still in need of a white suspect, police zeroed in on Chris Conover. When shown his picture in a photo array, Linda stated that he "resembled" the white man she had seen. She later selected him out of a lineup.

At trial, Conover presented numerous witnesses who testified that they had seen him at a birthday party at the time of the killings. In response, the prosecution presented the testimony of an FBI agent, who stated that microscopic examination of hairs found on Jordan's stepdaughter's body came from Conover. On May 23, 1985, Conover was convicted of two counts of murder, burglary, and related offenses and sentenced to life imprisonment.

After ten years in prison, the Innocence Project, a national litigation and public policy organization dedicated to exonerating the wrongfully convicted through DNA testing, accepted his case. In 2001, DNA testing conclusively proved that the hairs found at the crime scene belonged to two white men, neither of whom were Conover.

In 2001, DNA testing conclusively proved that the hairs found at the crime scene belonged to two white men, neither of whom was Conover.

Nevertheless, prosecutors continued to insist that Conover was guilty and threatened to retry him. In 2003, Conover came to an agreement with prosecutors, whereby he was released from prison in return for an "Alford" plea. By the terms of this plea, Conover maintained his innocence, but acknowledged that prosecutors had enough evidence to convict him. Thus, despite the physical evidence indicating his innocence, Conover has not been formally exonerated. While the deal was not ideal for Conover, he chose to accept it to spare his elderly mother's pain and alleviate the recurrent panic attacks he suffered in prison.

Chris with wife Sue

Upon his release in 2003, Conover lived with his mother and acquired a job as a title researcher from a childhood friend. He was married in 2004 to his high school sweetheart, Sue, who stood by his side throughout his conviction and release.

Unfortunately, prosecutors maintain that they did not make a mistake in charging Conover with murder. They attribute the DNA results to a lucky break and steadfastly maintain their belief in his guilt. As such, the hairs used to exclude Conover through DNA testing have not been run through the state's database of DNA profiles. Furthermore, DNA found in one of the victim's underpants has not been tested, despite the Innocence Project's stated willingness to pay all fees associated with the testing. As of 2009, no one else has been charged with the murders.

Letter / CHRIS CONOVER

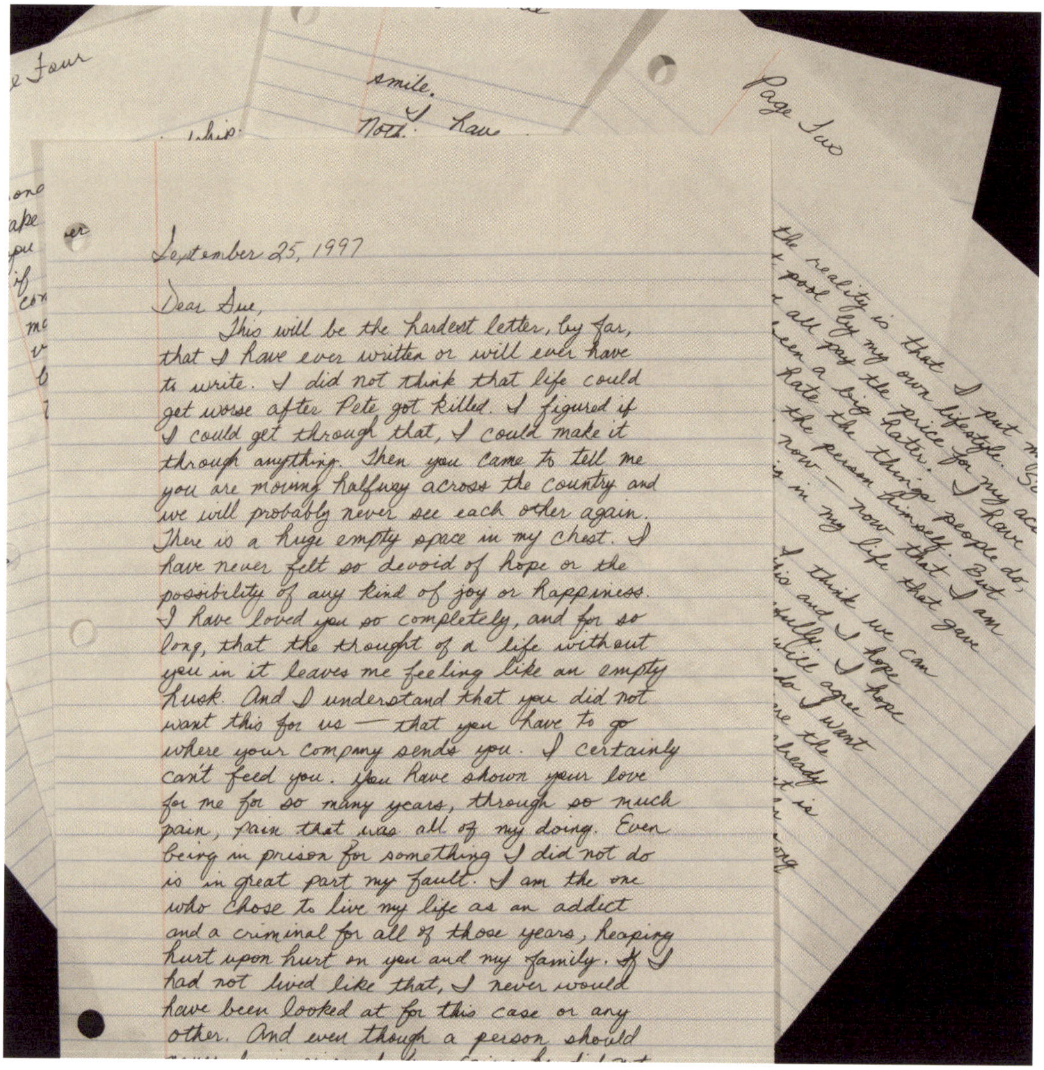

September 25, 1997

Dear Sue,

This will be the hardest letter, by far, that I have ever written or will ever have to write. I did not think that life could get worse after Pete got killed. I figured if I could get through that, I could make it through anything. Then you came to tell me you are moving halfway across the country and we will probably never see each other again. There is a huge empty space in my chest. I have never felt so devoid of hope or the possibility of any kind of joy or happiness. I have loved you so completely, and for so long, that the thought of a life without you in it leaves me feeling like an empty husk. And I understand that you did not want this for us — that you have to go where your company sends you. I certainly can't feed you. You have shown your love for me for so many years, through so much pain, pain that was all of my doing. Even being in prison for something I did not do is in great part my fault. I am the one who chose to live my life as an addict and a criminal for all of those years, heaping hurt upon hurt on you and my family. If I had not lived like that, I never would have been looked at for this case or any other. And even though a person should

This is a letter I wrote my girlfriend, Sue, in September 1997. We had been in love with each other since we were high school sweethearts, both 17 years old. In September 1972 I went to prison for most of the following 12 years, with a 4-month break in 1975. In 1984, just 8 months after my release and shorty after Sue and I became engaged, I was arrested and subsequently convicted of a double murder I did not commit. I was sentenced to three life sentences, plus 80 years without parole. Sue vowed to stay with me, which she did until I sent her this letter, begging her to move on and try to find someone to share the rest of her life with. She agreed to give it a try at first, saying that she did not want to live alone for the rest of her life. Two or three months later, I received [a] card from her and we have been together ever since. In July 2003, I was released through DNA evidence that excluded me as the donor of two crime-scene hairs. Sue and I were married in April 2004. As I said in the first paragraph of my letter, it was the hardest thing I ever wrote. As I read it today before getting it ready to mail, I cried over it once again.

September 25, 1997

Dear Sue,

This will be the hardest letter, by far, that I have ever written or will ever have to write. I did not think that life could get worse after Pete got killed. I figured if I could get through that, I could make it through anything. Then you came to tell me you are moving halfway across the country and we will probably never see each other again. There is a huge empty space in my chest. I have never felt so devoid of hope or the possibility of any kind of joy or happiness. I have loved you so completely, and for so long, that the thought of a life without you in it leaves me feeling like an empty husk. And I understand that you did not want this for us—that you have to go where your company sends you. I certainly can't feed you. You have shown your love for me for so many years, through so much pain, pain that was all of my doing. Even being in prison for something I did not do is in great part my fault. I am the one who chose to live my life as an addict and a criminal for all of those years, heaping hurt upon hurt on you and my family. If I had not lived like that, I never would have been looked at for this case or any other. And even though a person should never be imprisoned for a crime that he did not commit, the reality is that I put myself in the suspect pool by my own lifestyle. So now, once again, we all pay the price for my actions. I have never been a big hater. I have always tried to hate the things people do, rather than hate the person himself. But I truly hate myself now—now that I am losing the last thing in my life that gave me joy.

There is only one way I think we can make some good come of this and I hope you will consider it very carefully. I hope after considering it that you will agree with me. When you move to Colorado I want you to try to find someone to share the rest of your life with. You have already lost 25 years because of me and that is more than anyone should have to give for the actions of another, no matter how strong the love. When you move, I want you to consider yourself "available." I'm not asking you to go bar hopping—I know you wouldn't do that anyway. I am simply asking that you keep an open mind and if you should meet someone nice, you give him a chance. It is because I love you so much that I ask this of you. You deserve so much more than a life of accepting collect calls and getting repeat after repeat of the 5 "thinking of you" cards sold in the commissary. Pleasc smile.

I have so much guilt to live with, Sue. Nothing will ever let me escape my guilt about Pete. Yes, he was killed in a freak accident at work. But if he had not followed me into a life of drugs and crime, he wouldn't have been on such a lousy job in the first place, despite having 8 years clean. Maybe time will ease my pain in losing Pete—I doubt it will ease my guilt.

Maybe my guilt about you can be assuaged, at least a bit. If I were to hear that you had found a good man, a man that was good to you and good for you, it would make me so happy.

I love you so much and despite all of my faults and all of the wrong I have done, that love is pure and true. Pure and true enough that I could be happy knowing you were happy with another man. In fact, there is nothing I can think of that would make me happier. Please make this possible for me and more importantly, for you. Please tell me you will at least consider yourself open to a relationship if a worthy person should come along—that you will not feel bound by any obligation to me. Please.

I want this to be an amicable parting. I do not want to end our wonderful friendship. I don't want to take you off my visiting list in case you ever find yourself back this way. But if you force me to, I will stop all communication with you. Please don't make me do that. I do want you to visit me—I actually want you to bring a husband or serious boyfriend for my approval. If you love him, I promise you I will love him too. If he is good to you and makes you happy, he will have a friend for life in me.

You are probably thinking as I have thought—What if I get out? What if Barry Scheck pulls a rabbit out of the hat at this late date? Sweetie, we have to be realistic. The Innocence Project has been working on my case for two years now. They have money problems and my case seems to have stalled out. Unfortunately, that old saying "Hope for the best but expect the worst" fits perfectly here. I know they are trying hard for me and I do have hope but I also know the odds are about 100 to one for post-conviction relief in Maryland. My innocence has little to do with my chances. I have always believed that the police took hairs from my apartment and planted them or switched them with hairs from the crime scene. Look how they loaded the deck with my line-up: a 30 year old and 5 teenagers. That was no honest mistake. They believed I did this because of my past and they made sure I was convicted. You heard the FBI agent testify in court. The top hair and fiber expert in the world. He knew his business, which means the hairs were probably mine. If a DNA test is done, and the hairs were mine, who is going to believe me? You, my mom, and the guy who really did this.

No, I am not giving up hope, or quitting the fight. What I am doing is making a concession to reality and I need for you to do this, too. Please give yourself a chance. Knowing you are happy, with a good man to share the rest of your life with, would give me such peace.

I have said this the best way I could say it. I did not cry when my dad died or when Pete got killed. But my tears are staining these pages now. However, as hard as this had been to say, I mean every word of it. Please be with me on this, Sue. You know it is right.

Your Chris

DWAYNE ALLEN **DAIL**

SERVED 18 YEARS OF A DOUBLE LIFE SENTENCE

PLACE OF TRIAL
GOLDSBORO, NORTH CAROLINA

Courtesy of the Innocence Project
Researched by Andrew Cleves, Sean Martz, and Clement Tsao

On September 4, 1987, a man crawled through the window of a Goldsboro, North Carolina, apartment and raped a twelve year old girl who resided in the apartment. The girl identified Dwayne Allen Dail as her attacker and he was charged with burglary, rape, and other related charges. Hairs collected from the crime scene were submitted for forensic testing and an expert concluded that Dail's hairs were microscopically consistent with the evidence from the crime.

Dail reportedly turned down an offer to plead guilty in exchange for three years of probation. He went to trial in 1989. The evidence presented at trial included the victim's identification of Dail and the forensic testing showing the possibility that hairs found at the crime scene were Dail's. The jury found him guilty as charged and he was sentenced to a double life sentence plus fifteen years.

...all evidence introduced at Dail's trial had been returned to the Goldsboro Police Department and had subsequently been destroyed.

Dail filed numerous appeals and in 2001, the North Carolina Center on Actual Innocence (the Center) began working on his case. The Center is a non-profit organization dedicated to investigating post-conviction claims of actual innocence from unrepresented North Carolina inmates. Attorneys at the Center requested DNA testing on the evidence from Dail's case, but were told all evidence introduced at Dail's trial had been returned to the Goldsboro Police Department and had subsequently been destroyed. However, when the Center asked for a repeated search, officers found a box of evidence, including the victim's nightgown, that had been saved.

Officials at the Wayne County District Attorney's Office agreed to send the evidence for DNA testing. Semen matching another man already in prison was discovered on the victim's nightgown thus excluding Dail as the rapist.

Dail was released from prison on August 28, 2007, after a state court judge agreed to vacate his conviction and dismiss all charges against him. He was thirty-nine years old. He had spent half of his life behind bars. In October 2007, Dail received a pardon from the Governor of North Carolina, Mike Easley, based on Dail's actual innocence.

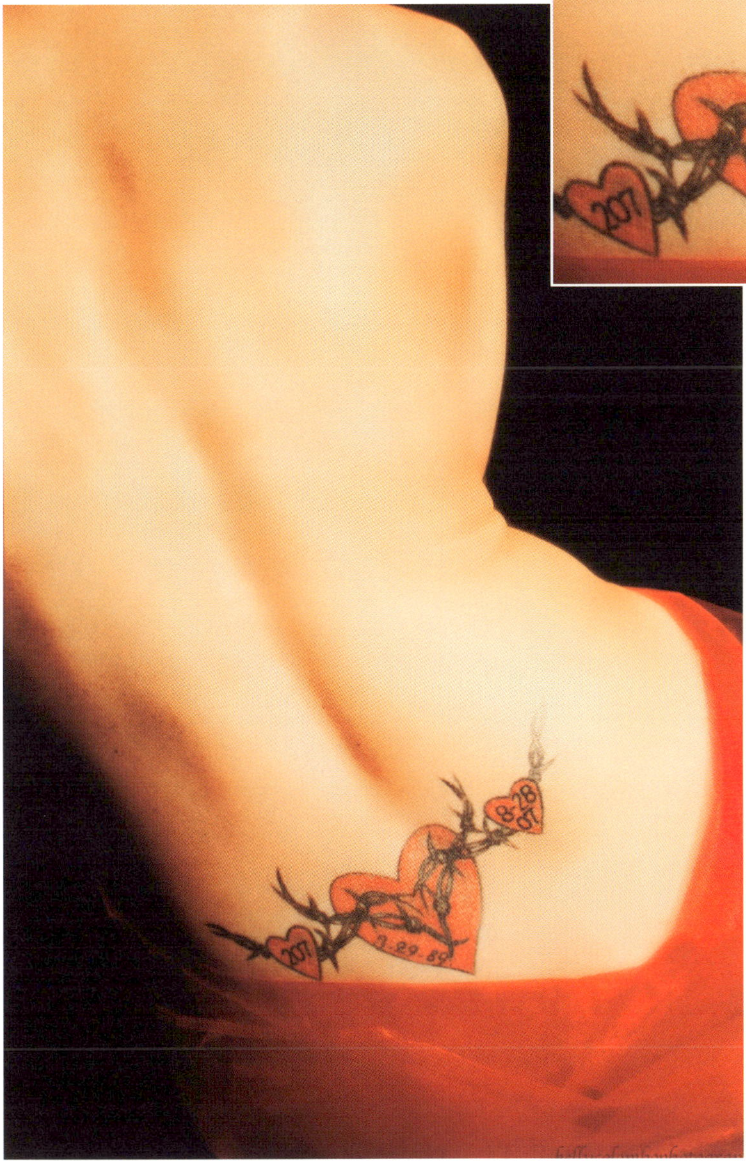

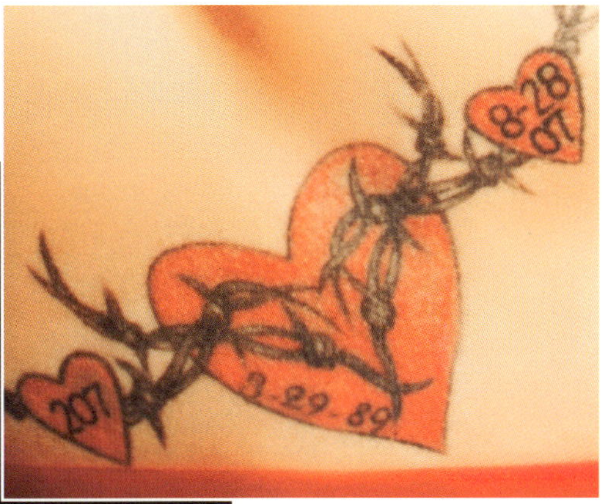

"Diana's Tattoo" / DWAYNE ALLEN DAIL

The tattoo represents the capture of Dwayne's heart, the hearts of his family members, and all of their freedom by the barbed wire of the prison. The date of Dwayne's conviction was added to the center heart when Dwayne's sister first got the tattoo, but she left the other two hearts blank with the hope that she could fill them in with the date of Dwayne's exoneration and his place in the ongoing DNA exoneration count, which was 207.

GARY DRINKARD

1995 2001

SERVED 6 YEARS OF A DEATH SENTENCE

PLACE OF TRIAL
DECATUR, ALABAMA

Written by Tiffany Allen
Researched by Julie Kathman and Ryan McGraw

On August 19, 1993, sixty-five year old automotive junk dealer Dalton Pace was found murdered at his home in Decatur, Alabama. He had been shot three times. The large amount of money Pace was known to carry had also been stolen.

On August 28, 1993, Gary Drinkard was arrested on an unrelated marijuana charge. Three days after his arrest, Drinkard was identified as the perpetrator of Pace's murder/robbery by Drinkard's half-sister and her common law husband who were both facing charges in an unrelated robbery. In exchange for implicating Drinkard, their pending criminal charges were dropped. Each stated Drinkard had informed them that he planned to murder Pace in order to rob him. Drinkard stayed in county jail for two years awaiting his trial.

> Despite being home at the time of the murders and with no physical evidence linking him to the crime, Drinkard was convicted...

At his trial in 1995, Drinkard was assigned two court-appointed lawyers: one who specialized in collections and commercial work and the other who represented creditors in foreclosure and bankruptcy cases. They failed to present physician-witnesses who would have testified that Drinkard's recent back injury made his committing the crime a physical impossibility. Despite being home at the time of the murders and with no physical evidence linking him to the crime, Drinkard was convicted of capital murder and was sentenced to death.

Two years after the Alabama Court of Criminal Appeals affirmed the conviction, the Alabama Supreme Court reversed and remanded the case for a new trial based on prosecutorial misconduct. In 2001, lawyers Richard Jaffe and John Mays working with the Southern Center for Human Rights (the Center), a non-profit organization that provides legal representation to people facing the death penalty, won him an acquittal. The Center later presented Drinkard to the United States Senate Judiciary Committee in order to illustrate the urgent demand for competent lawyers to be assigned to those facing the death penalty. Today, Drinkard lives and works in Cullman, Alabama, and is active in the movement to abolish the death penalty.

Photo courtesy of Witness to Innocence

"Love Me Now" / GARY DRINKARD

I wrote these while either depressed or angry to alleviate the depression or anger. I found that writing down silly words actually relieved my situation at the time. 26 Minutes is my favorite and did describe the process of getting someone ready to die in the electric chair.

If you're ever gonna Love me,

Better love me now!

I'll never see your face

In the free world, How?

I'm condemned to die

In a big electric chair

Where your soul can't rest

And your eyes only stare

The state said to "kill me"

Cause killing ain't good

And to bury me deep

In a plain box of wood

So if you're ever gonna love me

Better love me now

The people in this state

Just don't know how!

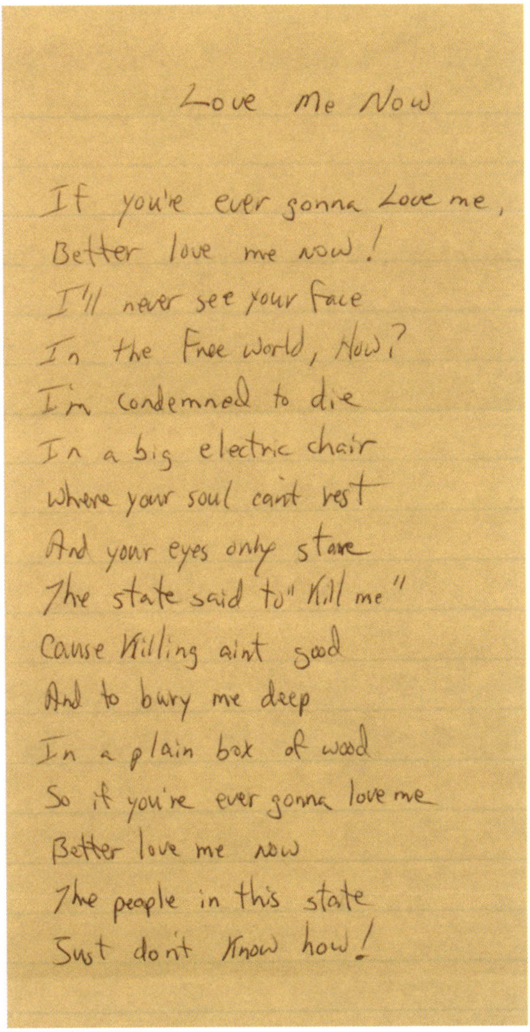
Love Me Now

If you're ever gonna Love me,
Better love me now!
I'll never see your Face
In the Free world, How?
I'm condemned to die
In a big electric chair
where your soul can't rest
And your eyes only stare
The state said to "Kill me"
Cause Killing aint good
And to bury me deep
In a plain box of wood
So if you're ever gonna love me
Better love me now
The people in this state
Just don't Know how!

"Twenty Six Minutes" / GARY DRINKARD

What are you gonna do
When they come for you
Death is only minutes away
you've counted your last day
sitting alone in the dark
smoking your cigarette's last spark
rough hands grabbing and reaching
man outside the cell preaching
slaps you on the head
Bends you over the bed
No diaper for you boy
Pain now, no more joy
Head buzzed clean with clippers
you'll wear socks not slippers
Rushing you out half airborne
Eyes filled with hate filled scorn
slamming you into the chair
Buckling you down with care
Here comes the head flap
Next is the legs strap
Damn! What you want to say
No calls ringing this way
fat man raises his hand
Lord plays his marching band
Come on home my son
Your time in this place is done
Zap...fizz...bang...once then twice
snake eyes on these dice
smoke billowing from your head
sure smells like you're dead!

What are you gonna do
When they come for you
Death is only minutes away
you've counted your last day
sitting alone in the dark
Smoking your cigarette's last spark
rough hands grabbing and reaching
man outside the cell preaching
slaps you on the head
Bends you over the bed
No diaper for you boy
Pain now, no more joy
Head buzzed clean with clippers
you'll wear socks not slippers
Rushing you out half airborne
Eyes filled with hate filled scorn
Slamming you into the chair
Buckling you down with care
Here comes the head flap.
Next is the legs strap
Damn! what you want to say
No calls ringing this way
Fat man raises his hand
Lord plays his marching band
Come on home my son
your time in this place is done
Zap ... Fizz ... bang ... once then twice

CLARENCE **ELKINS**

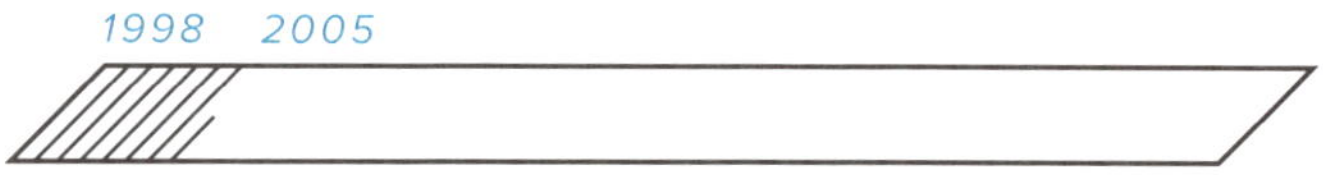

SERVED 7.5 YEARS OF A LIFE SENTENCE

PLACE OF TRIAL
SUMMIT COUNTY, OHIO

Written by Tiffany Allen
Researched by Julie Kathman and Ryan McGraw

In the early hours of June 7, 1998, Clarence Elkins' mother-in-law, Judy Johnson, and his six year old niece were brutally attacked by an intruder in Johnson's home in Summit County, Ohio. Johnson was beaten, strangled to death, and then raped. His niece was hit, sexually assaulted, and strangled to the point of unconsciousness, but survived. When his niece awoke, she went to a neighbor's house in order to get help and allegedly told the neighbor that her uncle, Elkins, was the one who attacked her and killed her grandmother. Hours after the attack, Elkins was arrested.

At trial, the prosecution theorized that Elkins killed his mother-in-law out of frustration because she was meddling in his rocky marriage to her daughter, Melinda. The case against Elkins was largely built on circumstantial evidence as investigators found no signs of forced entry, and no fingerprints or hairs linking Elkins to the scene. Elkins' alibi was also corroborated by neighbors and his wife who testified that he had been out with friends and then home at the time of the crime. Based on the testimony of Elkins' niece identifying him as her attacker, Elkins was convicted of murder, attempted aggravated murder, rape, and felonious assault. He was sentenced to life imprisonment.

Years after the attack, Elkins' niece recanted her statements and offered new details. She said her attacker's eyes were brown—Elkins has blue eyes. She also said her attacker wore cowboy boots and in a videotaped deposition, she said the killer was someone other than Elkins. Prosecutors believed the girl had been coached by her family members who wanted Elkins freed.

Years after the attack, Elkins' niece recanted her statements and offered new details.

▲ Clarence with sons

Clarence with wife Molly

In 2004, the Ohio Innocence Project took the case and had extensive DNA testing conducted. Male DNA that did not belong to Elkins was found in crucial locations on both victims (vaginal cavity of Johnson and panties of niece). Elkins' DNA was not found anywhere at the crime scene. Based on this new evidence, the Ohio Innocence Project sought a new trial for Elkins in a three-day hearing held in March of 2005. In July of 2005, the trial court denied the motion, effectively meaning that Elkins would have to spend the rest of his life in prison despite DNA test results proving that someone else committed the crimes.

Shortly after this troubling loss, the Elkins defense team learned of a new suspect, Earl Mann, a sex offender who resembled Elkins in appearance and who, it was discovered, had been staying in the neighborhood at the time the crimes were committed. Ironically, at the time this was discovered, Mann was an inmate in the same prison as Elkins. Alerted to this fact, Elkins acted as his own detective and collected Mann's DNA from a cigarette butt Mann had abandoned in a clean ashtray. After Elkins mailed the butt to a DNA lab, the results came back proving that Mann was the true perpetrator and confirming that Elkins was innocent.

...Elkins acted as his own detective and collected Mann's DNA from a cigarette butt...

On December 15, 2005, Elkins was exonerated and left prison a free man. Ten years after the crimes were committed, in 2008, Mann was convicted of the murder of Elkins' mother-in-law and of the attack on his niece. He is serving a life sentence without the possibility of parole.

Letter / CLARENCE ELKINS

Dad,

How are you? I hope that you are doing good. I can't even explain how much I miss you it is starting to get hard for me to deal with everything going on, I just sometimes can't believe what has happened to all of us. I Love you more than you will ever know. When I hear songs on the radio that remind me of all of the good times we used to share together it makes me feel good, but it hurts me at the same time. However I love to hear and see and remember the times that we had and the times that we will have soon. You are with me all of the time anywhere that I go, and everything that I do. It is hard for me to write down on paper what I am feeling. I hope that you understand what I am trying to say, but please don't worry about me too much because I always pull through on top of things just like you do, and I am proud of that. I am proud that you are my Dad, very proud of that. You give me direction and knowledge that someday I will be a Dad just like you were to me. One of these days. Anyway I went to the doctor he said I don't need surgery as of now, he wants me to start physical therapy in the water. I will be OK. I am going to send some pictures with this. I love you and everything will be OK. I always pull through so don't worry about me too much just keep praying for me and everybody and everything will be OK. Keep your head up. Keep faith. Love you. Miss you. Very much.

Love you,

Clarence II

P.S. July 6th oops June 6th we will be at the courthouse for that thing. Ya know. Love you keep your head up keep faith in God. Love you.

P.S. Angi said hi and Tim—

When you are incarcerated mail is our highlight of the day. This is one of the reasons I survived this horrific ordeal.

Wallet / CLARENCE ELKINS

Front & Back

The wallet was made while I was incarcerated in Mansfield prison. This was made out of leather shoes and trash bags. I sent both of my sons one for Christmas. It was the best I could do.

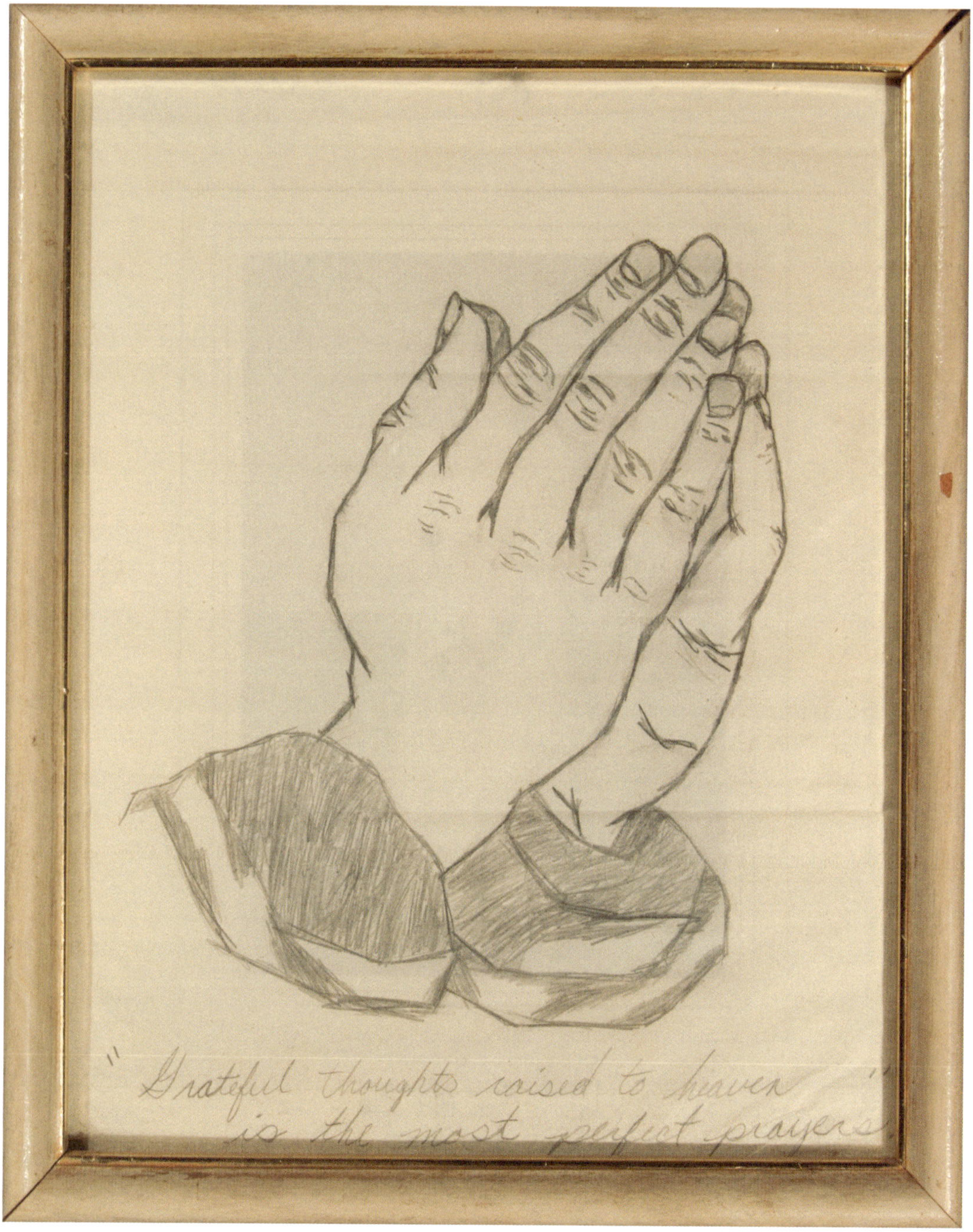

"Hands" / CLARENCE ELKINS

Picture of strength I had during my incarceration and I sent to my parents. I wanted my parents to keep the strength.

"Take Courage" / *CLARENCE ELKINS*

What though the day dawn gloomy?
Why should we feel despair?
Why should our hearts be heavy?
When Jesus is near, and doth care.

And when the dark clouds gather,
Why should we be dismayed?
Why should our hearts feel anguish?
When Jesus said, "Be not afraid."

Though fierce the tempest rages,
Why should we doubt and fear?
Why not trust the Rock of Ages?
Who told us to "Be of good cheer."

Tis joy to walk with Jesus,
No need from the tempter to flee,
For He who is stronger than Satan
Has promised our strength to be.

This poem I sent to my sons and spoke of my faith. I wanted to encourage them to stay strong. It speaks volumes of strength.

R. DEAN **GILLISPIE**

CURRENTLY SERVING 19 YEARS
OF A 16 TO 50 YEAR SENTENCE

PLACE OF TRIAL
MONTGOMERY COUNTY, OHIO

Courtesy of the Ohio Innocence Project
Researched by Megan Collard and Lindsey Fleissner

In August 1988, three women were raped in two separate incidents that involved forced oral sex in Montgomery County, Ohio. After the attacks, the victims helped police create a composite of their attacker.

After seeing the composite on a poster, a manager at a General Motors plant turned in the employee photo of one of his employees, Roger Dean Gillispie. Gillispie had no criminal record, but did not have a good relationship with management because he was considered a union agitator.

Although Gillispie's hair color and skin tone did not match the description of the perpetrator given by the victims, all three of the victims eventually identified Gillispie as their attacker. However, the photo of Gillispie used in the lineup stood out among the others—in Gillispie's photo, the background was bright yellow while the other photographs had blue backgrounds. Additionally, almost two years had passed between the time of the crimes and when the victims viewed the photo lineup raising doubts as to the strength of the victims' memories.

After he was arrested for these crimes, Gillispie adamantly asserted his innocence. He requested and passed a polygraph test and rejected a plea deal offered by the prosecution. The deal would have drastically reduced his sentence.

At trial, no forensic or other evidence linked Gillispie to the crime. In February 1991, Gillispie was convicted of multiple counts of rape, kidnapping, and aggravated robbery with firearm specifications. After his conviction, but before sentencing, new evidence was obtained and processed concluding that hairs taken from the victims did not match Gillispie. Gillispie moved for and was granted a new trial, but again he was convicted of multiple counts of rape. He was sentenced to sixteen to fifty years' imprisonment.

> [Gillispie] requested and passed a polygraph test and rejected a plea deal offered by the prosecution.

Since 2003, the Ohio Innocence Project (OIP), a component of the Rosenthal Institute for Justice at the University of Cincinnati College of Law that assists the wrongfully convicted, has been representing Gillispie, filing appeals and other motions on his behalf. Most recently, in July 2009, the Second District Court of Appeals ruled that the Montgomery County Court of Common Pleas must hold a hearing to consider new evidence regarding an alternative suspect in order to determine if Gillispie should be granted a new trial. The

Dean with his mother Juana and sister Jodi

alternate suspect not only perfectly fits the victims' descriptions of the perpetrator, but he committed copycat offenses with a very distinct modus operandi in the same area at the same time. In addition, the OIP's investigation uncovered that this suspect told others a series of the same distinct things that the perpetrator told the victims in Gillispie's case, such as that he is a contract killer by profession, that he is from Corpus Christi, Texas, and that he was molested by his grandfather when he was twelve years old, among other things.

That hearing was held over three days in the summer and fall of 2010. The OIP is currently awaiting the judge's decision as to whether Gillispie is entitled to a new trial on this ground.

Gillispie has now served more than nineteen years in prison for crimes he steadfastly asserts he did not commit.

In addition, the OIP convinced a federal court in Dayton, Ohio, to hold an evidentiary meeting on Gillispie's *Brady* claim. The *Brady* claim relates to the OIP's discovery that the original investigating officers had initially eliminated Gillispie as a suspect and written detailed reports to the file outlining their reasons. Later, after these officers retired, the detective who took over the case proceeded against Gillispie, and the exculpatory reports disappeared. The OIP learned of the reports from interviewing the original detectives, now retired.

Gillispie has now served more than nineteen years in prison for crimes he steadfastly asserts he did not commit. He has been a model prisoner, winning numerous awards and the respect of the wardens and administrators throughout the corrections system. Gillispie's friends and family doggedly stand by him in support of his innocence. Despite positive reports from prison, and from his life prior to being arrested, Gillispie was denied release by the parole board five years ago and again in 2010 because he refused to "accept responsibility." He simply declined, on grounds of principle, to admit guilt and present a case to the parole board of having been "rehabilitated" for crimes he did not commit. Today, Gillispie is still incarcerated at London Correctional Institution.

"The Native Cowboy" / R. DEAN GILLISPIE

Former Attorney General Jim Petro, now in private practice, joined the Ohio Innocence Project's team pro bono in 2008 shortly after leaving office to fight for Gillispie's exoneration. Dean Gillispie painted "The Native Cowboy" as a gift for Petro. The subject of the painting is a Native American man who is turning into a cowboy. The subject represents Dean's view of Petro as a lifelong prosecutor who turned into a defense attorney to assist in Dean's defense. On the back of the painting, Dean wrote:

It is a great honor and privilege to present this painting to Mr. Jim Petro, a man of the common working man and who has put forth a great effort to correct a wrong that occurred nearly twenty years ago.

Faith and encouragement has once again been restored to a family that had lost all but their prayers. They can now see a twinkle of light at the end of this long dark nightmare that gives hope that the truth will free an innocent man, their son.

This painting was done with heart-felt gratitude and personal integrity for a man who has and will continue to make a difference.

"As Long As There is One" / R. DEAN GILLISPIE

Dean Gillispie painted "As Long As There is One" in 2008 to motivate his attorney, Mark Godsey of the Ohio Innocence Project, as he approached his first evidentiary hearing in Dean's case. Since that time, Godsey and Jim Petro have represented Dean in three state evidentiary hearings, with a federal hearing scheduled for March 2011. It is the hope of Godsey and Petro that by the time this volume is published, Dean will be exonerated and freed. On the back of this painting, Dean wrote:

This painting of a warrior was painted by a warrior, "Dean 'Spiz' Gillispie" for a warrior, "Mark Godsey," who has fought, is fighting and will continue to fight for the innocent, as long as there is one.

Both images are copies of artwork by Jd Challenger. Reprinted with permission of the Jd Challenger Gallery.

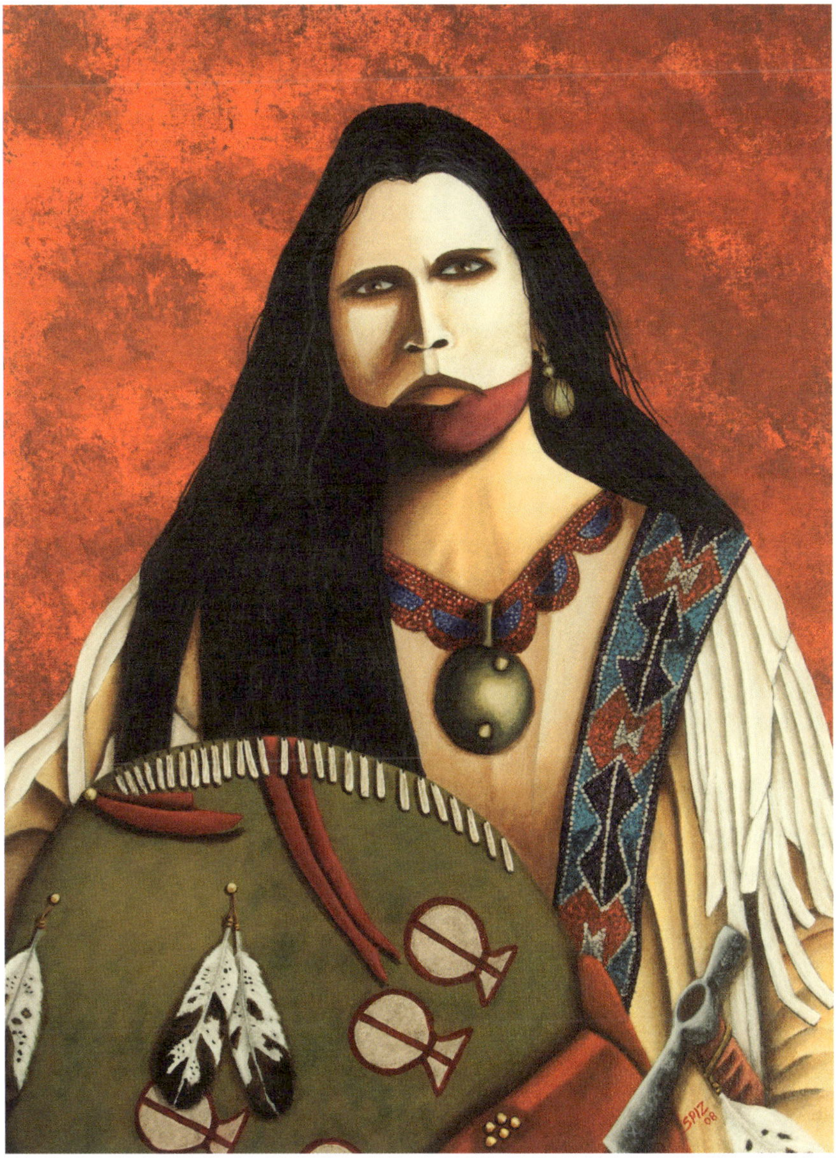

“A Stolen Life” / R. DEAN GILLISPIE

Front & Back

This painting represents my feelings about what the state of Ohio has done to my life.

The top left picture is me in 1991, when they “Stole my life.”

In the toilet painted in yellow (Urine Yellow) is the word LIFE, that’s my life being flushed down.

On top of that is a small list of things that are important in my life that I’ve missed. (A small list of the many great things).

The green represents assets, livelihood, and most important, Freedom.

The red heart represents the love of my life.

The orange represents some of the fun things I used to do.

The purple with gold wedding bells represents friends and family that have gotten married.

The black cross represents the deaths of friends and family.

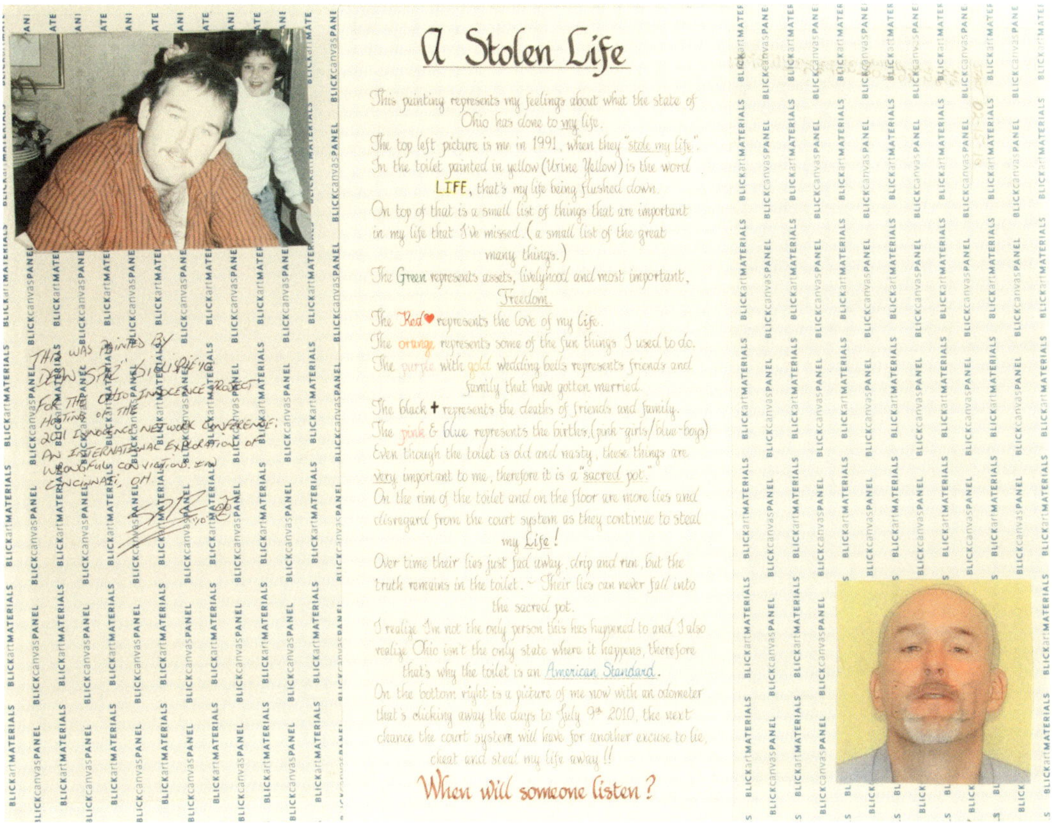

The pink and blue represents the births, (pink-girls/blue-boys).

Even though the toilet is old and nasty, these things are very important to me, therefore it is a "sacred pot."

On the rim of the toilet and on the floor are more lies and disregard from the court system as they continue to steal my Life!

Over time their lies just fade away, drip and run, but the truth remains in the toilet. Their lies can never fall into the sacred pot.

I realize I'm not the only person this has happened to and I also realize Ohio isn't the only state where it happens, therefore that's why the toilet is an American Standard.

On the bottom right is a picture of me now with an odometer that's clicking away the days to July 9, 2010 the next chance the court system will have for another excuse to lie, cheat and steal my life away!!

When will someone listen?

JEFFREY SCOTT **HORNOFF**

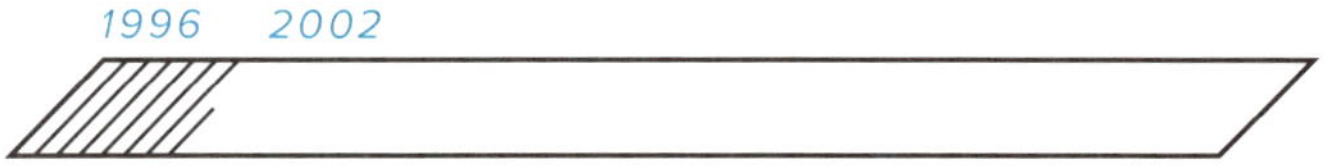

SERVED 6.5 YEARS OF A LIFE SENTENCE

PLACE OF TRIAL
WARWICK, RHODE ISLAND

Written by Megan McNeil
Researched by Jen Coy and Nathan Henegar

On August 11, 1989, Victoria Cushman was found in her Warwick, Rhode Island, apartment lying in a pool of blood. She had been bludgeoned to death with a seventeen pound fire extinguisher found near her body. During the summer of 1989, Jeffrey Scott Hornoff, a twenty-seven year old Rhode Island Police Detective, had been intimate with Cushman irrespective of the fact that he was married. Hornoff had recently ended the affair, but Cushman wanted to keep it going as was evidenced by an un-mailed letter found at Cushman's apartment stating as much. When Hornoff was questioned by police as to his relationship with Cushman, he initially denied the affair in order to shield it from his wife. He later acknowledged the affair after spending an hour with police interrogators who knew the contents of the letter.

There was no physical evidence of any kind or any witnesses linking Hornoff to the murder.

At the time of the murder, Hornoff was at a party with his wife and friends. There was no physical evidence of any kind or any witnesses linking him to the murder. People at the party confirmed his presence and Hornoff took and passed a polygraph test to show he was innocent even though polygraph tests are inadmissible at trial. A grand jury that considered the evidence against Hornoff was dismissed without indicting him. However, in 1991, the Rhode Island State Patrol took over the investigation after the police department was accused of protecting one of its own.

In 1994, Hornoff was indicted by a second grand jury. At trial, prosecutors dismissed Hornoff's alibi claiming that he slipped away from the party, murdered Cushman, and then returned without anyone noticing his absence or the state his clothing would have been in had he just bludgeoned someone to death. The un-mailed letter was presented as circumstantial evidence of his motive even though there was no evidence that Hornoff even knew about it, as was his initial claim of only having had a platonic friendship with the victim. There were no fingerprints, no blood evidence, no DNA evidence, and no witnesses linking Hornoff to the crime.

On June 19, 1996, Hornoff was convicted of first-degree murder and was sentenced to life imprisonment. In 1999, Hornoff appealed the conviction and requested a new trial from the Supreme Court of Rhode Island. His request was denied. Hornoff maintained his innocence and, with the help of the New England Innocence Project, an organization that provides pro bono legal assistance to inmates who have claims of actual innocence, and the National Police Defense Foundation, sought DNA testing in an effort to finally prove his innocence. On November 1, 2002, Todd Barry, consumed with guilt, walked into the Rhode Island Attorney General's office and confessed to murdering Cushman. In exchange for pleading to second degree murder, he was given a thirty year sentence with fifteen years suspended.

Scott with children in Afghanistan where he is serving as an international police officer

Five days after Barry confessed, Jeffrey Scott Hornoff, then forty years old, walked out of the courthouse a free man. He was later exonerated by the same judge who had presided over his initial trial and was reinstated to the police force with back pay and benefits. Hornoff waived his right to the back pay in order to settle his civil lawsuit against the state so that his children would benefit from a statute allowing the children of police and firefighters to obtain tuition waivers for state universities.

On November 1, 2002, Todd Barry, consumed with guilt, walked into the Rhode Island Attorney General's office and confessed to murdering Cushman.

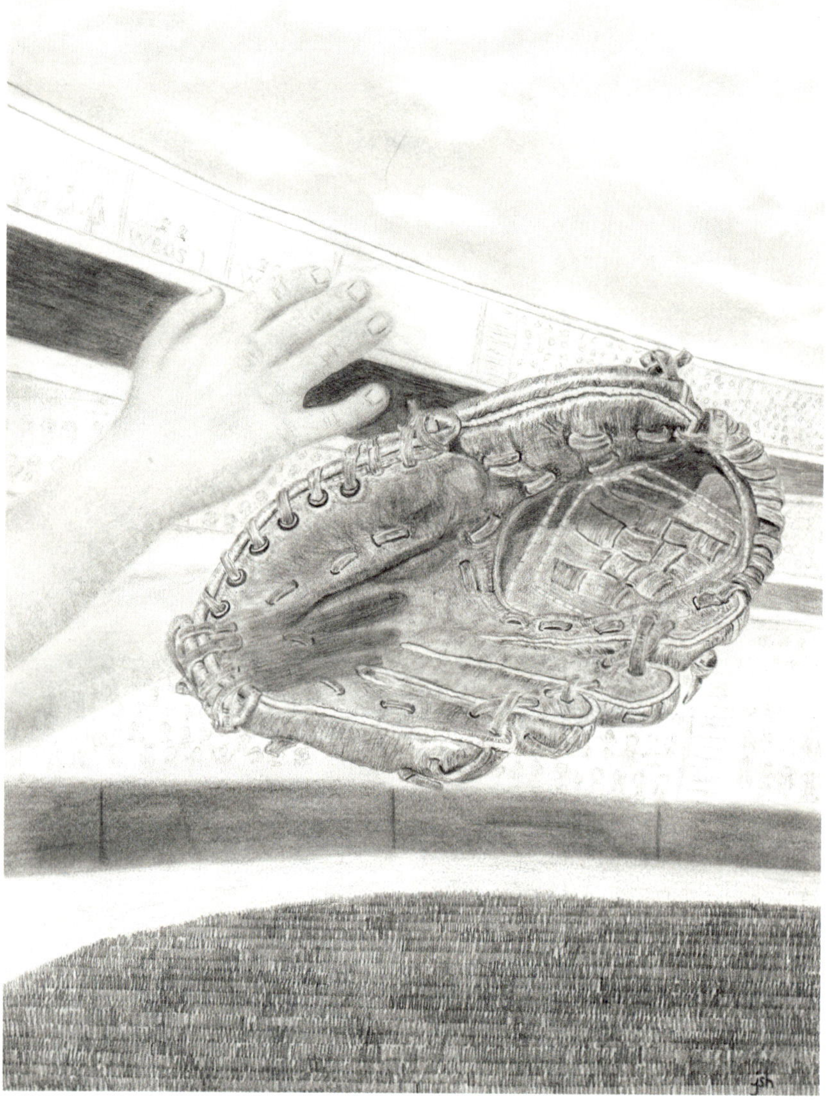

"Field of Dreams" / JEFFREY SCOTT HORNOFF

Drawn with #2 pencils and toilet paper

I had ordered the book 'Drawing Realistic Textures in Pencil,' by J.D. Hillberry, and the images of the hands playing catch are in this great book.

These were the most difficult drawings I did. I was forced to start over a couple of times due to my tears ruining the paper. As I drew my hand with the background of the ballfield I grew up playing at, then my son, Jacob's, hand, with a big league stadium behind his, I thought of the end of the movie 'Field of Dreams,' where Kevin Costner's character gets to play catch with his Dad's ghost. I wondered if I'd ever have a chance to play catch with my son who was born three months after I went to prison.

I met J.D. Hillberry at an art show following my release (can't remember when or where), but he recalled seeing my drawings based on his book (either Dateline or American Justice profiles), and he seemed almost as glad to meet me as I was to meet him. June 2002.

jsh

"A Prayer for Peace" / JEFFREY SCOTT HORNOFF

My oldest brother, Ron, discovered through researching genealogy that we have some Native American blood running through our veins. This drawing represents my dream of a peaceful spirit since mine was in such turmoil. It is also indicative of my connection with my ancestors and the freedom they enjoyed, as well as the vast expanse of the canyon in the background and the soaring eagles overhead. August 2002.

"Square Holes, Round Peg" / *JEFFREY SCOTT HORNOFF*

If ever I prayed for a life alone,

Single again and on my own;

Never did I mean to inherit this,

Divine interventions, my pleas amiss.

For, stripped of liberty and of three sons,

For another's crime the nightmare runs;

Full gauntlet here amid foul dregs,

An outsider in square holes, a round peg.

'Square Holes, Round Peg' was penned after another night of being surrounded by many men I had little in common with except my current situation. I didn't consider myself better, just different. But I also tried not to judge because, for all I knew, some were innocent too, there were a couple I fully believe were innocent. I had returned to my cell, hoping for a little quiet, but the men in segregation above me were yelling/communicating through the vents, banging on their desks, going crazy...so, that was my inspiration.

"Once Home" / *JEFFREY SCOTT HORNOFF*

Once home I go,
then you'll know
my fears and my pain;
Never to roam, I'll show,
these scars of woe,
and tears I once refrained.

My restless mass
here stirs and waits,
a prisoner in this cell;
Till these days pass,
if it's my fate,
oh, stories I will tell.

Or could it be
my destiny
to age with time
in here?
Then would my plea
to set me free
but chime
on only deaf ears?

'Once Home' was another poem I wrote with no particular person to send it to, just writing so I could concentrate on something else for a little while — maneuvering different words around until I felt it was understandable. Just trying to place myself outside my present and into a better future.

"For My Son Jacob" / *JEFFREY SCOTT HORNOFF*

I am the daddy you don't know,

As you age, as you grow;

Two years and a half now you are,

In another world, as I fight this war.

When I dream of my return,

Much to do, so much to learn.

Though chains of foe keep us apart,

Always here inside my heart.

Silent tears one day shall dry,

Then reunited, you and I;

To laugh, to hug, to smile and sing,

And lose ourselves on dragon's wing.

Each year I wrote a birthday poem for each of my sons. As far as 'For My Son Jacob', I tried to keep it upbeat and positive, imagining being with him, moving forward and forgetting about everything we missed.

TIMOTHY **HOWARD**

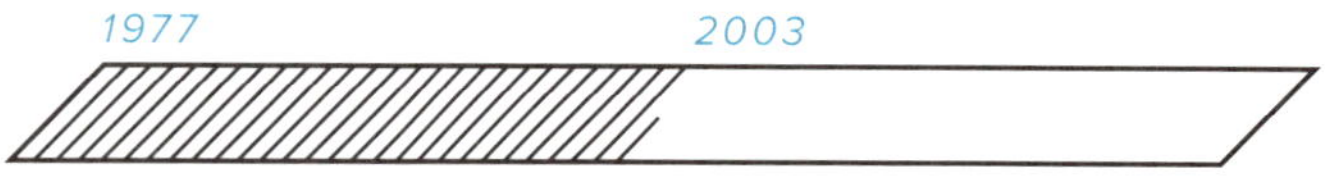

SERVED 26.5 YEARS OF A LIFE SENTENCE

PLACE OF CRIME
COLUMBUS, OHIO

Courtesy of Centurion Ministries
Researched by Lauren Creditt and Hilly McGahan

On December 21, 1976, two men robbed an Ohio National Bank in Columbus, Ohio. One man fatally shot the security officer and the other leapt over the counter and grabbed money from inside the teller's cage. The day after the crime an informant told police that they should question Timothy Howard. As soon as Howard heard that he was wanted for questioning, he immediately went down to the police headquarters to clear his name. That was his last day of freedom until April 23, 2003. Howard and a childhood friend, Gary James, were both convicted of aggravated murder and robbery. Howard's only brush with the law prior to December 1976 was possession of a stolen bicycle as a juvenile and a marijuana possession charge that was dismissed.

The testimony presented by prosecutors at Howard's trial in 1977 included that of an eyewitness to the crime and a Columbus police officer who dusted the crime scene for fingerprints. The police officer testified that he was unable to lift any fingerprints in the area touched by the cage-jumper, although in fact he had lifted fingerprints that didn't match either Howard or James. The eyewitness against Howard was an FBI informant, Robert Simpson, who owned a used tire store across the side alley from the bank. He claimed that he got a good look at one of the two fleeing bank robbers who ran past his store. He identified Howard as that man. Simpson told the jury that he had personally known Howard from the neighborhood because Howard had been in his store on a number of occasions.

Heavily relying on this testimony, the jury convicted Howard of aggravated robbery and aggravated murder. He was sentenced to death. In 1978, his sentence was commuted to life in prison when Ohio ruled capital punishment was unconstitutional.

In 1996, Centurion Ministries, a secular non-profit organization that works to free the convicted innocent throughout the United States and Canada, began to work on behalf of Howard and his codefendant Gary James. Centurion Ministries and two Columbus-based attorneys were able to prove that the eyewitness and the police officer perjured their testimony at Howard's trial. Through its investigation, Centurion Ministries discovered that the prosecution suppressed the police report regarding the fingerprints found at the crime never revealing it to the defense at trial.

Heavily relying on this testimony, the jury convicted Howard of aggravated robbery and aggravated murder. He was sentenced to death.

Thanks to the assistance of a retired FBI agent, Centurion Ministries was also able to obtain an un-redacted FBI report summarizing the interview with Simpson immediately after the crime, in which Simpson stated that he did not recognize either of the two fleeing bank robbers.

Photo courtesy of Diane Bladecki

When the presiding judge of Franklin County set aside Howard's conviction and freed him in April 2003, Howard had spent more than half of his life in prison. During Howard's twenty-six and a half years of incarceration, his father died, his mother contracted colon cancer, one of his sons was shot in a drive-by shooting, and two grandsons were born. Howard's codefendant, Gary James, was exonerated in July 2003.

Upon release, Howard began working in a barbershop with his son, a licensed barber. In 2005, Howard received a $2.5 million settlement from the state of Ohio, $1.1 million of which he was to receive in monthly installments over the next thirty years. In March 2007, Timothy Howard died of a heart attack at the age of 53, having spent exactly half of his life behind bars.

In March 2007, Timothy Howard died of a heart attack at the age of 53, having spent exactly half of his life behind bars.

"After Cezanne" / TIMOTHY HOWARD

"Hands" / *TIMOTHY HOWARD*

"American Eagle" / TIMOTHY HOWARD

LEE WAYNE **HUNT**

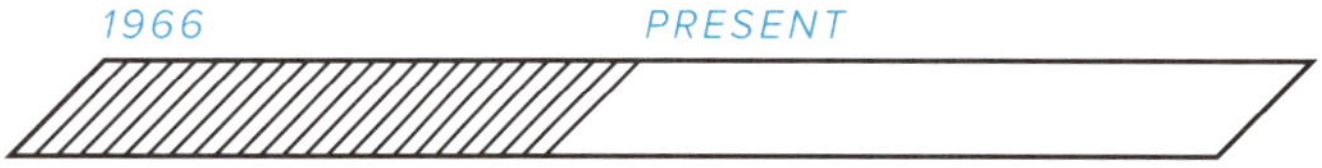

CURRENTLY SERVING 24 YEARS
OF A DOUBLE LIFE SENTENCE

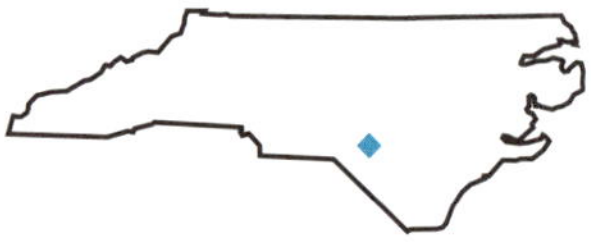

PLACE OF CRIME
FAYETTEVILLE, NORTH CAROLINA

Courtesy of Richard Rosen, University of North Carolina School of Law
Researched by Nicole Billec, Joseph Lehnert, and Amanda Rieger

The murders of Roland and Lisa Matthews took place on March 7, 1984, in Fayetteville, North Carolina. They were both shot and stabbed. Their two year old son was found unharmed in a bedroom. Within weeks of the murder investigation, police focused their attention on Lee Wayne Hunt, a known drug dealer, and Jerry Cashwell, as possible suspects. Police ran a comparison of Hunt and Cashwell's fingerprints with those found at the murder scene, but no matches were found. Police then began to question Eugene Williford, a career criminal and acquaintance of Hunt and Cashwell's, as a possible participant in or a witness to the murders. Despite repeated questioning, Williford claimed to know nothing about the murders, at least for the time being.

In December 1984, Williford was arrested for numerous offenses and failed to make bond. As a result, Williford and his attorney began extended negotiations with police. On February 22, 1985, Williford gave a statement to police implicating himself, Hunt, and Cashwell in the murders. A month later, Williford gave another statement adding Kenneth West as a participant. In return for his statements and future testimony against Hunt and Cashwell, prosecutors gave Williford total immunity for his alleged participation in the Matthews' murders and for all other pending charges.

The primary evidence used against Hunt at his trial in 1986 was the testimony given by Williford who claimed that he drove Hunt and West to the victims' home where they met Cashwell and committed the murders. A jailhouse informant also testified that Hunt made statements while in jail that suggested his personal knowledge of the murders and that Cashwell had made statements supporting Williford's version of the crime.

No blood, fiber, or other physical evidence linked Hunt to the crime scene. The only physical evidence used in the case was "lead batching" evidence—now discredited by the FBI—linking the bullet fragments found at the murder scene to a box of bullets traced to Cashwell, thus corroborating Williford's testimony. Hunt testified at trial on his own behalf admitting that he was a drug dealer, but he denied having anything to do with the murders. He also testified that Cashwell confessed to committing the murders. Hunt's lawyers subpoenaed Cashwell as a witness, but Cashwell refused to testify, relying on his Fifth Amendment right not to incriminate himself. Hunt was convicted of a double murder in 1986 and sentenced to consecutive life sentences.

No blood, fiber, or other physical evidence linked Hunt to the crime scene.

After obtaining convictions against Hunt and Cashwell, the State allowed West, the third person implicated by Williford in the murders, to enter a plea to accessory after the fact and conspiracy charges in return for a three year active sentence plus probation. During this proceeding, however, the State made West swear to a version of the events on the night of the murders that was materially different from the evidence introduced at Hunt's and Cashwell's trials.

On August 28, 2002, Cashwell committed suicide in prison. After Cashwell's suicide, Cashwell's defense attorney, Staples Hughes, disclosed Cashwell's confession that he alone had murdered the Matthews and that Hunt had nothing to do with the crime. Hughes believed his disclosure was appropriate based on a recent court decision that held the attorney-client privilege does not protect the confidentiality of communications if the disclosure did not harm the deceased, his estate or his family. *In re Miller,* 585 S.E.2d 772 (N.C. 2003). Hughes believed Cashwell's confession based upon his experience as a defense lawyer; Cashwell's hatred for Hunt; and the fact that the confession, even to his lawyers, was harmful to the way in which the lawyers could conduct Cashwell's representation.

Responding to Hughes's disclosures, professors Richard Rosen and Kenneth Broun of the University of North Carolina School of Law agreed to represent Hunt in his claim for a new trial. They sent an investigator to search for Williford and to talk to West and Goodman. Williford died before the investigator could locate him. After first acknowledging that Williford's testimony had been false, West refused to talk further to Hunt's lawyers without his own representation. When contacted, Goodman continued to insist that Hunt had made a statement to him, but claimed that he did not understand Hunt's statement to be a confession to participation in the crime.

Rosen and Broun subsequently filed a motion for appropriate relief (MAR) on Hunt's behalf based primarily on Hughes' disclosures. The MAR also raised issues concerning the "lead batching" testimony and the inconsistent theories put forward by the State at

Professors Richard Rosen and Kenneth Broun of the University of North Carolina School of Law agreed to represent Hunt in his claim for a new trial.

Hunt's trial and at the sentencing of West. On January 8, 2007, a hearing on the MAR was held before the Cumberland Superior Court. Despite the clear holding of *Miller*, the court ruled Hughes' testimony was barred by the attorney-client privilege. Cashwell's other defense attorneys also refused to testify in light of the court's ruling on the attorney-client privilege. Hunt attempted to question West as a witness, but West refused to testify after both the Court and the State refused a request that he be granted immunity from prosecution for perjury.

Consequently, on April 24, 2007, all of Hunt's claims were denied. The judge also referred Hughes' conduct to the North Carolina Bar, but the Bar dismissed all claims of misconduct without a hearing. Exhausting all state court remedies, a habeas corpus petition is now pending before the United States District Court for the Eastern District of North Carolina. On May 6, 2008, the North Carolina Innocence Inquiry Commission accepted Hunt's case for review and their inquiry is pending. Former North Carolina Chief Justice, I. Beverly Lake, Jr., has joined in Hunt's request for review in the North Carolina Supreme Court and in his federal habeas corpus petition.

"Letter to Mom" / LEE WAYNE HUNT

Dear Momo,

I hope this letter will find you feeling better, and with a very big smile on your face today. I hope you can feel my love all in your heart, because we know love is always the best thing we can give to our hearts. I wanted you to know that I'm thinking about you today. And I want you to know that I'm doing very good thanks to our loving God, and all of the love and care he is always giving to me. Momo you are always with me even when we are apart, and whenever we are apart and I'm feeling so all alone, I can close my eyes and think of all the good and happiness we had knew together, and a smile will always come on my face and I can feel your love all in my heart. Then I can see in my mind how your loving smile is always such a precious sight to me and to my heart! Your hugs was always so comforting and so very right! I think of how I could always be myself around you. And how you always made so much in life seem all so wonderful and good! And somehow I always felt so much better because I could then clearly see your love that I will always hold us dear within my heart forever and ever! You are always in my heart with me. I love you with all of my heart and soul. Momo I hope and pray you can always feel my love running all in your heart. I pray that my love will make your heart work better, and will work for years to come, because you are the one that keeps our family together. Momo I know you have always taught me that all things are always in God's hands, and that He will always do the right things, but know that I will keep praying very hard for God to make your heart better. I always knew that you live every day to go home to be with God, but I still pray that it is not your time to go home to be with God. Momo I know that I've always been a very hard headed kid, and I give you a very hard time and I would worry you. Momo I'm so sorry for being so hard headed and you know that you taught me to always tell the truth, and to always be good those that you can. And you have always knew that I'm in this prison for something I didn't do, and one day they will talk to God about their lies, because I want you to know that I did forgive them, and put this in God's hands! And I don't want you to ever worry about me because I'm in Gods hands now. And you can tell by the love that I'm sending to you in this letter. And if you goes home to be with God before I get out of this prison, I will see you when my time come to go home to be with our Lord Jesus Christ the Great Creator. I will see you there OK. So one day we will be together again! So Momo don't worry about me, because God is taking very good care of me. I will be all right because I'm in Gods hands. And you know that he is going to take very good care of your hard headed son! I got a letter from Jeannette, and she tell me that she is also sick. And I wrote her back, and I hope my letter will make her smile, and I hope she can feel the love that I'm sending her way. You know that I always loved Jeanette, because she was always a very caring and loving woman. I pray that the love I'm sending her in this letter will help her get better. Jeanette also tells me that Aunt Nancy wanted me to write her, so I'm going to write her today also. You know that I've always loved Aunt Nancy and Uncle Pete. Momo I'm going to say goodbye for now but know that I will write you back next week OK. I want you to know that I love you with all of my heart and soul and I wish I could be there with you now.

Momo I love you so very much,
Your loving son, Lee Wayne Hunt.

Written on November 27, 2003 for my dying mother
And she went home to be with God on December 6, 2006

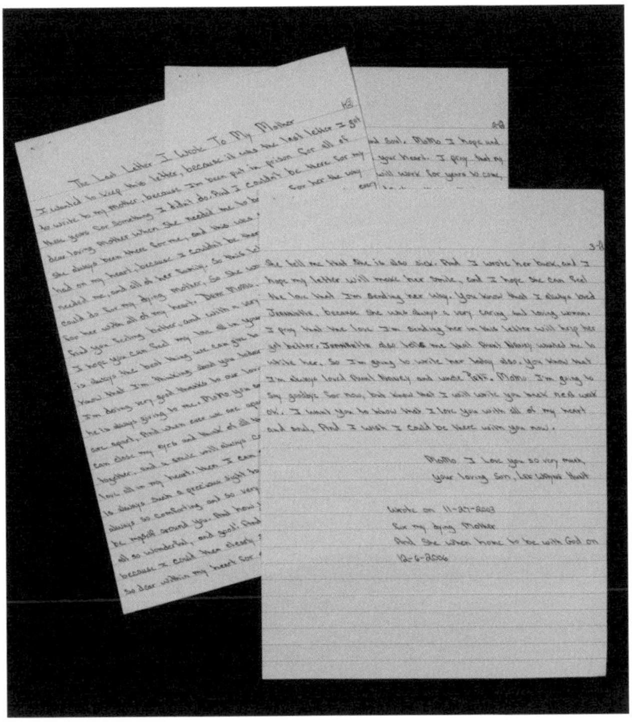

She tell me that she is also sick. And I wrote her back, and I hope my letter will make her smile, and I hope she can feel the love that I'm sending her way. You know that I always loved Jeannette, because she was always a very caring and loving woman. I pray that the love I'm sending her in this letter will help her get better. Jeannette also tells me that Aunt Nancy wanted me to write her. So I'm going to write her today also. You know that I'm always loved Aunt Nancy and uncle Pett. Momo I'm going to say goodbye for now, but know that I will write you back next week OK. I want you to know that I love you with all of my heart and soul, And I wish I could be there with you now.

Momo I Love you so very much,
your loving Son, Lee Wayne Hunt

Wrote on 11-27-2003
for my dying Mother
And She when home to be with God on
12-6-2006

I wanted to keep this letter, because it was the last letter I got to write to my mother, because I've been put in prison for all these years for something I didn't do. And I couldn't be there for my dear loving mother when she needed me to be there for her the way she had always been there for me, and this was the hardest thing I've ever had on my heart, because I couldn't be there for my mother when she needed me, and all of her family. So this letter was the only thing I could do for my dying mother, so she would know that I loved her and cared for her with all of my heart.

RON KEINE

1974—1978

SERVED 4 YEARS OF A DEATH SENTENCE
WAS 9 DAYS AWAY FROM THE GAS CHAMBER

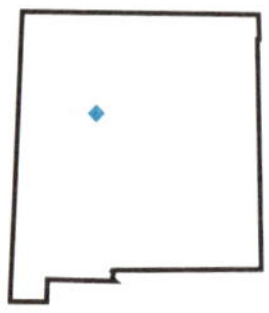

PLACE OF CRIME
ALBUQUERQUE, NEW MEXICO

Written by Jennifer Miller
Researched by Guy Cardamone and Claire Gutmann

On February 6, 1974, University of New Mexico student William Velten, age twenty-six, was murdered and his mutilated body was hidden in brush on the side of the road in Albuquerque, New Mexico. Ron Keine, a member of a motorcycle gang passing through the area a week after the crime occurred, was arrested by police on an unrelated charge. Keine, along with three friends, were later convicted of the kidnapping, rape, murder, and mutilation of Velten and were sentenced to death.

An investigation later conducted by the *Detroit News* uncovered a conspiracy by prosecutors to create a case against the defendants. Prosecutors theorized the murder had taken place at a motel, and they, along with the police, coerced testimony from one of the motel maids, Judy Weyer, to support their argument. Police told Weyer they would help her boyfriend get out of jail if she agreed to testify. Weyer made statements about a group of suspicious motel tenants she thought could be connected to the crime, but denied any actual knowledge of the murder. To pressure her to testify against Keine, police threatened to charge her with perjury (even though perjury can only take place in court) and implicated her boyfriend in the murder. Police then arrested Weyer and charged her as an accessory. After two weeks in jail, Weyer fabricated an elaborate story in which she stated she had been raped by the defendants and was forced to watch as they murdered and mutilated Velten.

An investigation later conducted by the *Detroit News* uncovered a conspiracy by prosecutors to create a case against the defendants.

Despite a confused story by Weyer, dated receipts showing Keine was not in town at the time of the crime, witnesses corroborating Keine's alibi, and a lack of any physical evidence, the jury convicted Keine of the kidnapping, rape, murder, and mutilation of Velten. He was sentenced to death. After the trial, when the prosecution refused to release Weyer's boyfriend, Weyer retracted her story in a series of taped newspaper interviews. After the story broke, a New Mexico judge still refused to grant a new trial. The tapes mysteriously disappeared.

In the fall of 1975, Kerry Lee—the real killer of William Velten—had a religious epiphany and confessed to the murder. Lee presented intricate knowledge of the murder and an accurate hand-drawn map of where the body was hidden. Maintaining Lee's story was not believable, prosecutors did not file charges against him. It was not until information provided by Lee led to the recovery of the murder weapon that a judge quashed the murder indictments against Keine, nine days before he was to be sent to the gas chamber. Lee was tried and convicted of the murder in 1978.

Photo taken by Sofia Moro of El Pais, courtesy of Witness to Innocence at witnesstoinnocence.org

Since his exoneration, Keine has become an active leader in the anti-death penalty movement. He currently lives in Detroit where he owns his own business. He has given numerous speeches about his wrongful conviction throughout the United States to educate others about the flaws in the American justice system and why the death penalty should be abolished.

Since his exoneration, Keine has become an active leader in the anti-death penalty movement.

"Collateral Damage" / RON KEINE

One of the most overlooked and seldom mentioned effects of the death penalty is the horrible victimizing of innocent people. This collateral damage is most disheartening when one looks at the immediate family of the death row denizen. What they suffer through is truly cruel and unusual.

Even though I was Innocent—exonerated after two years on death row after the confession of the law enforcement officer who was the real murderer—my family suffered greatly.

My mother would not come out of the house for two years because of peer pressure. She had a son on death row. Even her closest friends did not know how to greet her at the super market, drug store or on the street. What do you say to a mother who is grieving as the state prosecutor gets to kill her son? It will not be alright. Time will not heal these wounds. Tomorrow or next week or next month will not be better. Others, mostly strangers, but also a few so called friends were not so kind to her and did not remain silent.

She quit church when someone sitting in the back row of pews loudly called out, "Murderer. Rapist." As she walked out of that church, in tears with her shawl over her head in shame, she probably never heard the people admonishing the loud mouth.

She was shunned by the local society that had, in the past, respected her and relied on her outgoing personality to bolster the morale at community and social gatherings. She became a recluse. Even after I was exonerated she remained so. She died in sadness, never recovering her love of life and former status as a pillar of our community. I wonder if she ever understood that she shunned society more than they shunned her. My grandmother was a little stronger. She, at least, went to church. Some say that Grandpa went to church only to defend Grandma from the ridicule. I think it was so he could argue with people who talked about me, and so he could shake his ever present cane at them. I really loved that old man. He taught me how to fish.

Execution is not a death such as a car accident. Or a sudden mishap or an accidental death. A death that can be easily forgiven or excused. This killing is slow and calculated. It takes an average of ten years to execute a man and they start killing him the day he is put on death row. The anticipation of one's own death day after day is immeasurably horrifying. Throughout the appeals, which last many years and cost an average $3,200,000.00 per person, I wonder if families of the executed are aware of the indignity of even having to pay for that death with their tax dollars. Several times these men were innocent and the family knew it.

My father planned his suicide for months. He was saved, just in time by the news of my exoneration. A few days later and the state would have got a death anyway as he had already purchased the gun.

Probably the worst effects of all were inflicted on my kids.

Peer pressure is perhaps the most profound on school age children.

Children can be cruel and outright vicious. "Your daddy is a Murderer." "Your daddy rapes people." "They should have killed him."

"How do we know he did not do it?" "My dad says that your dad got out because of a slick lawyer." "My mom says she better not see him at any school functions or she will give him a piece of her mind." "Our parents are watching him when he is around kids." This all happened even though my daughters were born years after my release. I would get that phone call from the school to come and pick up a daughter as she was in distress because of the harassment. As she sat crying, waiting for me to leave work to come and get her. She didn't know that I was also wiping the tears off my face. Some times I would have to sit in the school parking lot for a few minutes so I could compose myself before entering the building. I had to be strong for her.

These were innocent little girls. What did they ever do to deserve this? How can God let this happen to them? It became an ordeal to make them go to school every day. They shuddered at the thought of it. Changing schools (six times) worked only for a short time until the punishment started again. They never did graduate. They both quit when they became old enough to do so. What a total waste of human minds.

One of the girls has an IQ of about 160.

My only thanks is that this did not happen when I was on the row. They did not have to live through the debacle of a justice system that is allowing the state to kill their daddy. Thousands of other innocent children were not so lucky. I wonder what it is like for them to have to carry that burden. I wonder how mothers answer that much dreaded question, "Why do they have to kill my daddy?"

The Collateral damage piece came as a result of my reading an article about what victims families go through. I wanted people to understand that that the hurt, the tears, the damage is also prevalent and usually much worse on the other side if the issue.

Ron Keine

GLORIA **KILLIAN**

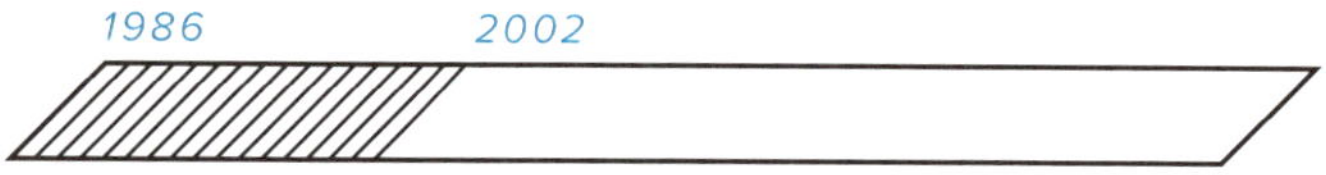

SERVED 16 YEARS OF A 32 YEARS TO LIFE SENTENCE

PLACE OF TRIAL

SACRAMENTO, CALIFORNIA

Written by Kamiikia Alexander
Researched by Kayla Delk and Jessica Lantaff

In December of 1981, cousins Gary Masse and Stephen DeSantis broke into the home of a Sacramento, California, couple. During the course of the robbery, one of the victims was shot and killed. Shortly after the crime, authorities received a telephone call that implicated Masse and DeSantis as the perpetrators. Masse's wife told authorities that Gloria Killian, a casual acquaintance of Masse, had planned the robbery. Police questioned Killian, a former law student with no criminal record, but foreclosed the possibility of her involvement in the crime. Masse turned himself over to authorities and was convicted of first degree felony murder. Masse was sentenced to life without the possibility of parole.

Soon after his conviction, Masse contacted authorities in order to strike a deal to lower his sentence. Prosecutors offered Masse a sentence reduction in exchange for his testimony concerning the other parties involved in the robbery and murder. Masse implicated Killian and DeSantis whom were both arrested and charged. Although DeSantis testified that Killian did not participate in the planning or commission of the crime, with Masse as the key witness for the prosecution, Killian was made to stand trial.

At trial, Masse testified that Killian devised the plot, accompanied him to the home of the couple during a prior robbery attempt, and demanded proceeds from the December robbery. Masse also claimed that he was not receiving a leniency deal in exchange for his testimony even though the prosecutor involved in the case sent a letter to a Sacramento trial judge endorsing a sentence reduction for Masse. Subsequently his sentence was reduced to life with the possibility of parole. Based on Masse's testimony, Killian was convicted of first degree felony murder, robbery, and conspiracy. She was sentenced to thirty-two years to life.

Following Killian's conviction, Masse wrote several letters that revealed he lied about Killian's participation in the crime. The letters were discovered after many years by DeSantis's attorneys as DeSantis sought to challenge his death sentence. The letters were given to Killian's appellate lawyer who submitted them to a federal magistrate judge raising the issue of perjury.

Following Killian's conviction, Masse wrote several letters that revealed he lied about Killian's participation in the crime.

Despite Masse's admission that he lied about Killian's participation in the crime and the proof that Masse received a sentencing deal, the federal magistrate recommended that Killian's conviction be upheld. The Court of Appeals for the Ninth Circuit did not agree and, in March 2002, reversed her conviction holding that it was based upon false testimony offered by the prosecution's key witness, Masse.

Killian plans to complete law school and help other inmates in similar situations.

After serving sixteen years, Gloria Killian was released from prison in 2002. She was exonerated with the assistance of Joyce Ride, the mother of astronaut Sally Ride, who paid for the services of her appellate lawyer. Killian plans to complete law school and help others who were wrongfully convicted.

"Forget Me Not" / GLORIA KILLIAN

We are incarcerated women

We are the forgotten, the marginalized, the dispossessed, the abandoned

The disposable refuse of a throw-away society

But the consequences of our repudiation have been overlooked in society's haste

To hide its social and moral problems behind barbed wire and bars of steel

For we are the mothers of the future generations

The children who were torn from our arms

Will grow up to share the lessons they learned in their youth

As they have received, so shall they give

Those who were beaten, will inflict violence on others

Those who were sexually abused, will prey upon the innocent

The homeless and unwanted will become destroyers

The addicted will spread their sickness through out the land

But those who received love, will give love to others

Those who received help, will one day help others

Compassion will be shared in the measure that it was received

Children who were permitted to bond and heal with their imprisoned mothers

Will grow up to make positive contributions to society

They will not sow the pain and anger of those who could never heal

Women who were helped to rehabilitate themselves

Will teach their children

To recover from their wounds

To be strong

To be kind

And to rise above their circumstances

Bitterness or blessing

The choice is yours

WE ARE YOUR FUTURE

I wrote this in 1992 during a time when there was a huge backlash against women with children. We were experiencing a trend in which women were losing their children to foster care under a "fast track system" instituted in California.

“A Different Time and Space” / GLORIA KILLIAN

The concepts of time and space have very different connotations for incarcerated women, then for other people. It is undoubtedly true that every individual who is imprisoned measures time by the length of their sentence, but for women the markers are more personal and painful. Time is measured in the weeks, months, and years by which a woman is separated from her family. It is measured by the hours and days between letters and phone calls. Time is measured by the birthdays, holidays, and personal events that she misses. The first tooth under the pillow, the new trike, and the first day of kindergarten are little pieces of time in her children’s lives that she can neither share nor recapture.

Incarcerated women who are lucky enough to have visits with their families can see the passage of time in their children’s faces, the sudden growth spurt, or the new hairdo. In the Visiting Room mothers and children try to recapture those missed moments with stories, hugs, laughter, and tears. In that noisy, crowded room families try desperately to re-establish bonds and create new ones to bridge the gaps in lives that were torn apart by the mass incarceration of mothers, daughters, sisters, aunts, and grandmothers. There is never enough time in the Visiting Room.

Women who do not receive visits from their families measure time by the photographs they receive and the letters and pictures that their children send. Each treasured photograph, and scrawled crayon drawing is proudly displayed to everyone the mother knows, even the guards. The scraps of paper and faded photos carefully taped to an inmate’s locker bear silent witness to the passage of time in which a mother and her child are kept apart.

For women whose children have been placed in foster care, time is measured by the months between court appearances and her desperate efforts to fulfill the court ordered reunification plan. Often times the woman’s sentence runs longer than the period of time that she has been granted to get her life back together so that she can regain custody of her children. Failure to fulfill the court ordered reunification plan results in the termination of parental rights and the adoption of the children. In these cases time cuts both ways as it marches on: too much time in prison, too little time to get the children back.

Time drags in prison as the women wait for the days to pass. They wait to go to meals, to sign up for the phone, to be called to a visit, to be allowed into and out of their cells, to go to Canteen, to go to Clothing, or to go to work. They wait to be assigned to school, a better job, or a self help program that can make a difference in their lives. They wait for good news, good times, and a new life. Time passes on and still they wait.

In prison there is always too much time, but sadly there is never enough space. Women in California prisons live 8 women to one cell, crammed into a tiny space about the size of a bathroom, sharing one toilet and one shower. They exist literally on top of each other; 4 women on top bunks, 4 women on bottom bunks, with their meager possessions stuffed into a drawer beneath the bottom bunk. There is no space to breathe, to think, to grieve, or to grow. There is no space to heal wounds, to make amends, to find peace, or to seek a better way. Everywhere a woman goes in prison she is surrounded by crowds of inmates and dozens of guards. Space does not exist in prison.

Yet as time drags on in prison, the women worry about both time and space. Will there be a space for me in my children's lives when I am released? A space in my mom's house? A space in my husband's heart? Is there space for me anywhere or has it been destroyed by the time that I have lost behind these concrete walls?

I wrote this in response to a request and I was annoyed that there was so little understanding in the world about the deprivation that women in prison experience.

RAY KRONE

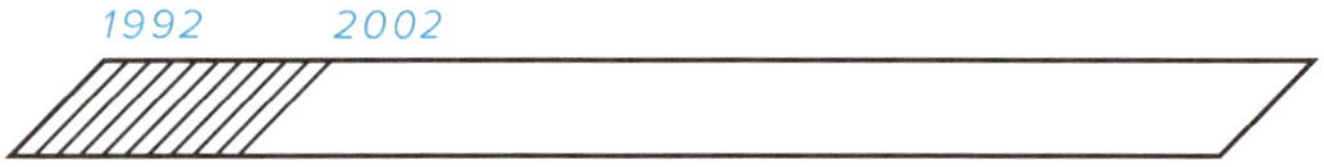

SERVED 10 YEARS OF A DEATH SENTENCE

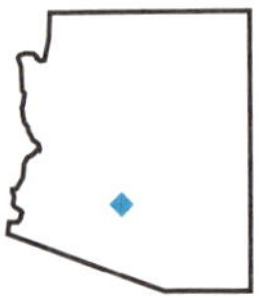

PLACE OF CRIME
PHOENIX, ARIZONA

Courtesy of the Innocence Project
Researched by Patrick Bradley, Lauren Creditt, and Hilly McGahan

On the morning of December 29, 1991, the body of thirty-six year old Kim Ancona was found lying nude, in the men's restroom of the Phoenix, Arizona, bar where she worked. She had been fatally stabbed. The perpetrator left behind little physical evidence—blood at the crime scene matched the victim's type, and saliva found on her body came from someone with the most common blood type. There were no fingerprints or semen and no DNA tests were performed.

During the attack, Ancona had been bitten on her left breast and neck with enough force to leave teeth marks. Upon hearing Ray Krone, a regular customer, was to help her close the bar that night, investigators asked Krone to make a Styrofoam impression of his teeth for comparison. The impression appeared to match the bite marks on Ancona. On December 31, 1991, Krone was arrested and charged with murder, kidnapping, and sexual assault.

At his 1992 trial, Krone maintained his innocence, claiming to be at home asleep at the time of the crime. Experts for the prosecution, however, testified that the bite-marks found on the victim's body matched the impression that Krone had made on the Styrofoam and a jury convicted him of murder and kidnapping. He was sentenced to death and a consecutive twenty-one year term of imprisonment. Krone was found not guilty of the sexual assault. He spent two years and eight months on death row in Florence, Arizona, watching other condemned inmates taken away for execution.

The judge sentenced Krone to life in prison, citing doubts about whether or not Krone was the true killer.

Krone won a new trial on appeal in 1996, but was convicted again, mainly on the state's supposed expert bite-mark testimony. This time, however, the judge sentenced him to life in prison, citing doubts about whether or not Krone was the true killer.

It was not until 2002, after Krone had served more than ten years in prison, that DNA testing proved his innocence. DNA testing conducted on the saliva and blood found on the victim excluded Krone as the source and instead matched a man named Kenneth Phillips. Phillips was incarcerated on an unrelated sex crime and, although he had lived a short distance from the bar where the victim worked, he had never been considered a suspect in her murder.

On April 8, 2002, Krone was released from prison. On April 24, 2002, the District Attorney's office filed to formally dismiss all charges against him. Murder and sexual assault charges have since been brought against Phillips.

Photo courtesy of Witness to Innocence

Ray Krone spent more than a decade in prison, some of it on death row, before DNA testing cleared his name. He is the 100th former death row inmate freed because of innocence since the reinstatement of capital punishment in the United States in 1976. He was the twelfth death row inmate whose innocence has been proven through post-conviction DNA testing. Prior to his arrest, Krone had no previous criminal record, had been honorably discharged from the military, and had worked in the postal service for seven years.

Krone was the twelfth death row inmate whose innocence has been proven through post-conviction DNA testing.

"To My Friends and Family" / RAY KRONE

Because of you – I can continue to be
full of Hope, and Faith, and Dreams you see.
Because of the support and encouragement given in love
my heart and spirit soar high above.

It's been many years since we've shared the same space
and spent time together and spoke face to face
The wonders I've witnessed serve to comfort my soul
and seeing you all once again is my ultimate goal.

So please don't worry—what will be—will be.
I pray for our Lord to bless you as He surely has me.
For only from the power that comes from above
could any one person be shown so much Love—

Thank you with all my heart.

Ray Krone

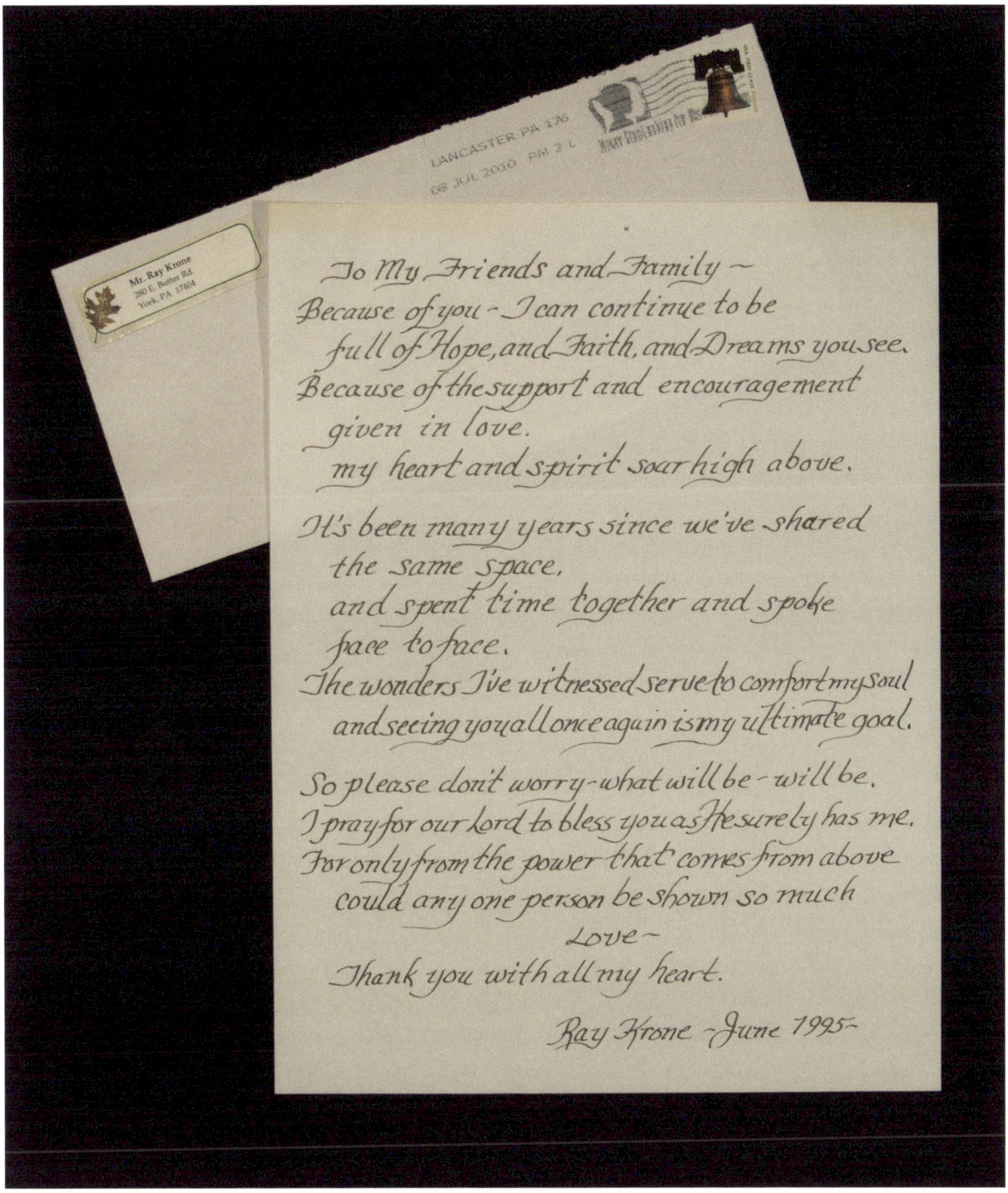

To My Friends and Family ~
Because of you - I can continue to be
full of Hope, and Faith, and Dreams you see.
Because of the support and encouragement
given in love.
my heart and spirit soar high above.

It's been many years since we've shared
the same space,
and spent time together and spoke
face to face.
The wonders I've witnessed serve to comfort my soul
and seeing you all once again is my ultimate goal.

So please don't worry - what will be - will be.
I pray for our Lord to bless you as He surely has me.
For only from the power that comes from above
could any one person be shown so much
Love ~
Thank you with all my heart.

Ray Krone ~June 1995~

I wrote this poem of thanks to those who had stood by me and believed in my innocence. It was written from my cell on Arizona's death row just after receiving the long awaited direct appeal response from the AZ Supreme Court who had just overturned my conviction and ordered a new trial for me. After 3 years on the row, I was going to get another chance to prove my innocence. I knew how much this also meant to my family and friends and wanted to thank them and ease their worries. We had all been carrying such heavy burdens for so many years.

LARRY **LAMB**

CURRENTLY SERVING 17 YEARS OF A LIFE SENTENCE

PLACE OF CRIME

MOUNT OLIVE, NORTH CAROLINA

Courtesy of Christine Mumma, Director, North Carolina Innocence Project
Researched by Nicole Billec, Whitney Frazier, and Amanda Rieger

In the early morning hours of February 28, 1987, Leamon Grady, a local bootlegger, was murdered in his home in Mt. Olive, North Carolina, by a single gunshot wound to his chest. His wallet, commonly known to be full from his bootlegging sales, was stolen. Grady's murder was unsolved for over five years, when a "witness," Lovely Lorden, having heard about a reward for information relating to the murder and who was concerned that her former abusive boyfriend, Bo Jones, was getting ready to be released from prison, approached police and implicated her former boyfriend in the murder.

> Lorden received $4,000 for her statements, which changed with each account she gave regarding the night of the murder...

Lorden received $4,000 for her statements, which changed with each account she gave regarding the night of the murder; eventually Lorden incorporated Larry Lamb and Ernest Matthews as accomplices in her story. Another paid witness, and a friend of Lorden's, provided additional incriminating statements against Lamb. There was no physical evidence in the case or logical connection between Bo Jones, Larry Lamb, and Ernest Andrews.

Six years after the murder, Lamb turned down a plea deal to testify against Jones and was sentenced to life in prison. After Lamb and Jones were convicted, Matthews pled guilty and was sentenced to twenty years. He has since been released.

In 2006, Jones' writ of habeas corpus was granted and his 1993 convictions were vacated on the grounds that his trial counsel rendered ineffective counsel at both the guilt/innocence and sentencing phases of trial. The judge further found that Lorden's statements were "riddled with inconsistencies" and that "Lorden [was] unable to fairly and reliably describe the circumstances of the offense." Before Jones' retrial, Lorden signed two affidavits completely recanting her prior statements and trial testimony. As a result, the district attorney had no choice but to file a dismissal in Jones' case.

Since Jones' dismissal, Lorden has recanted the recantations of her prior testimony. The North Carolina Center on Actual Innocence, a non-profit organization dedicated to investigating post-conviction claims of actual innocence from unrepresented North Carolina inmates, is currently representing Lamb in his fight to regain his freedom that was lost through the use of paid and coached informants.

"Wrongfully Convicted and Incarcerated" / *LARRY LAMB*

"Many people in society feel that being incarcerated is more like a vacation with all the expenses paid. Being incarcerated is a hard life with many struggles. Many aspects of the department of correction are totally opposite from what these people think. We have to push and push hard to get the bare minimum of health care. In most cases it will take several months before you get to see a surgeon or specialist to diagnose your problem. Often times our family members have to call Raleigh or the Superintendent of the facility to see why we're not being treated. A large percentage of the officials whether it be, (medical staff, case managers, programmers, kitchen staff, or the officers that work in the dorms) are very unprofessional. It is easy for them to classify all inmates as the same. We don't all belong in the same category.

Once one is incarcerated he or she must choose which path they will travel. The negativity is always present. The Nascar race, basketball, football pools, and gambling is a path that many travel. This path leads to one inmate trying to get over on another inmate, fighting, homosexuality, and the many schemes inmates try to play on the officials. These activities lead to write ups, segregation, the loss of good time, and even the loss of custody levels. Those that travel that path most likely will be incarcerated most of their adult life.

I chose to travel the positive path doing what I thought would help me in the future. In 1995 when my sister Betty died, although I was able to attend her funeral handcuffed to an official I had to remain positive. When my mother died in 2002 and I was not allowed to attend her funeral, I had to remain positive. I was granted a private viewing of my mother's body without any of my family members allowed to be there. That was the coldest feeling I have ever experienced yet I had to remain positive.

After seventeen years and ten months of incarceration I have remained infraction free. By carrying myself in a positive manner I have earned the respect of many inmates and officials as well. During this era of my life God has allowed me to be an inspiration to many and some an inspiration to me. I have shared my favorite concept with many, that is, being incarcerated is what you make it to be, the choice is yours.

Excerpt from Larry Lamb's essay, "Wrongfully Convicted and Incarcerated"

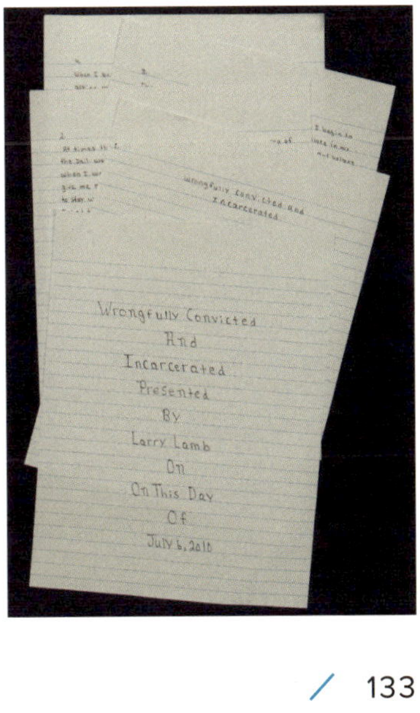

WALTER **LOMAX**

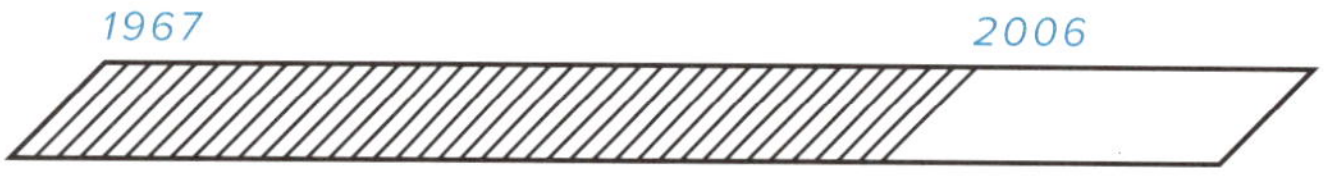

SERVED 39 YEARS OF A LIFE SENTENCE

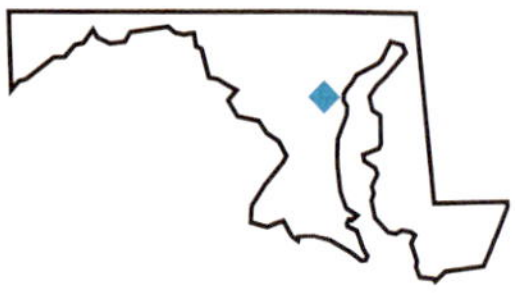

PLACE OF CRIME

BALTIMORE, MARYLAND

Courtesy of Centurion Ministries
Researched by Jen Coy, Nathan Henegar, and Megan McNeil

On December 2, 1967, a gunman robbed and fatally shot the owner of the Giles Food Market, a convenience store, in Baltimore, Maryland. Under pressure to solve multiple crimes in the area, police resorted to *en masse* lineups of young black men at the police station which were advertised in the local newspaper. Seventy-five witnesses to fifty-eight crimes, including the Giles Food Market murder, arrived at the police station to view the line-ups.

While at the police station, Walter was mistakenly put into one of the numerous line ups.

During this same time period, Walter Lomax learned that there was a warrant out for his arrest. He voluntarily went to the police station to see why he was wanted. The warrant was actually for his brother for non-payment of child support. While at the police station, Lomax was mistakenly put into one of the numerous line ups. He was cross-racially misidentified by three people who saw the Giles Food Market shooting. Neither of the two clerks who had a clear and calm view of the perpetrator identified Lomax as the robber/shooter.

Lomax's actual innocence was established by his physical condition on the date of the crime. Nine days before the crime, Lomax was stabbed in his right hand during a struggle with a gang of attackers. Lomax's stab wound was incurred in such a forceful manner that the knife went through his hand partly severing a portion of the muscles, fracturing a bone, bursting blood vessels, and causing significant swelling. He also suffered severe rib and chest damage during the attack.

Immediately following the attack, Lomax was rushed to the hospital and a plaster of Paris cast was applied from his palm and fingers to his elbow. Lomax returned to the hospital multiple times including on the day of the crime as the swelling in his hand worsened. According to Lomax's friends and family, his painfully bruised ribs restricted his movement to such an extent that he could barely move during his first week of rehabilitation. His friends and relatives were never presented at trial by his counsel.

Unfortunately, Lomax's trial attorney did not present the hand injury in a way that the jury could understand.

All of the witnesses to the crime described the perpetrator as wielding and shooting the gun in his right hand without any difficulty. None of the witnesses noticed anything unusual with the shooter's right hand. Police chased the criminal in full flight and saw him evade a police cruiser and an officer. Additionally, the perpetrator had purchased and carried in each hand, two large shopping bags of groceries that he took outside before reentering the store to commit the crime. Lomax could not have done these things given the extent of his chest and rib injuries and his severely injured right hand.

Unfortunately, Lomax's trial attorney failed to present evidence concerning the circumstances of Lomax's hand injury. Both the judge and jury were left puzzled as to how Lomax received the injury. Defense counsel also failed to mention the rib and chest injuries. On January 14, 1969, Lomax was convicted of first degree murder and was sentenced to life imprisonment. He was also convicted of two counts of robbery and sentenced to imprisonment for terms of ten and twenty years to run concurrently with the life sentence.

On December 13, 2006, Lomax, then 59 years old, walked out of the same courtroom in which he was convicted four decades earlier, but now as a free man.

Thirty-nine years after Lomax's conviction, Centurion Ministries, an organization that works to free the convicted innocent throughout the United States and Canada, filed a motion to reopen the post-conviction case and suspend the life sentence to time served. In granting the motions, the court made reference to the "evidence of actual innocence," as well as Lomax's spotless thirty-nine year prison record. On December 13, 2006, Lomax, then fifty-nine years old, walked out of the same courtroom in which he had been convicted four decades earlier, but now as a free man.

"Soliloquy with Malcolm" / WALTER LOMAX

Malcolm my man, I sho-nuff like talking with you, it seems like after we're through I always know exactly what to do.

It's getting rough though, people beginning to think something's wrong, they think I am standing here talking to myself, beginning to whisper, "Maybe the Cat ain't still strong."

Malcolm I know just what you meant, and I can see that you had your hands full. Now life still ain't no joke brother, in fact the load is harder to pull.

What's done happen is tranquility done set in, the tranquilizer ain't coming from without no more, it's coming from within.

I shouldn't be surprised though, because you told me in the beginning things wasn't right, but brother you could have at least pulled my coat to the type of people I was going to have to fight.

Now don't misunderstand me, I am not giving up the struggle, because I know that there are a lot of innocent people caught out there in the jungle. It's just that I am uptight this morning, and getting off on you, cause you're the Black shinning prince, and where I turn when lost for what to do.

By Walter Mandela Lomax 1980

'Soliloquy with Malcolm' was written in 1980 during a transformation in my life. As you may be aware, I was serving a life sentence for a crime I did not commit and this was a period of awakening for me.

BILL MACUMBER

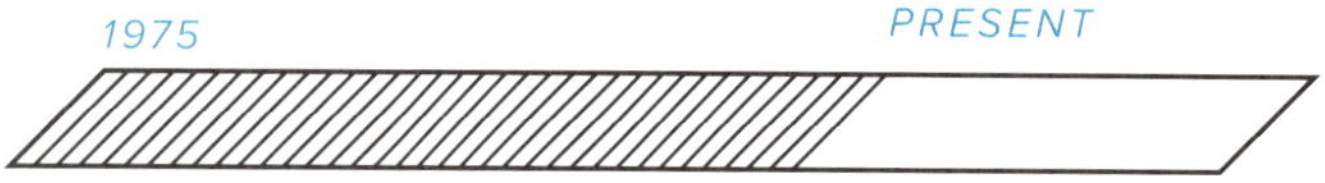

CURRENTLY SERVING 35 YEARS
OF TWO LIFE SENTENCES

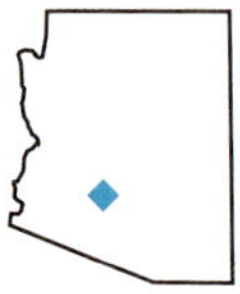

PLACE OF TRIAL
MARICOPA COUNTY, ARIZONA

Written by Kamiikia Alexander
Researched by Kayla Delk and Jessica Lantaff

On May 24, 1962, the bodies of Tim McKillop and Joyce Sterrenberg were found in an open desert area in Maricopa County, Arizona. Both victims had been shot in the head and were lying near Sterrenberg's car.

Investigators from the Maricopa County Sheriff's Office (MCSO) recovered shell casings, a handkerchief, and thatch of human hair from the scene. Tire tracks and various footprints thought to belong to the killer were also found. An MCSO deputy lifted several latent fingerprints from the vehicle after it had been towed for processing.

In September of 1962, a seventeen year old girl named Linda Primrose told investigators that she had witnessed the murders. According to Primrose, she had ridden with a female and several men, including Ernie Valenzuela, to a desert area to look for a stash of drugs. When they encountered another car near the drug stash, Valenzuela argued with the male and female occupants of the car and eventually shot and killed both of them. Primrose also successfully led officers to the scene of the crime and passed a lie detector test.

Valenzuela confessed to the murders on multiple occasions in 1964 and to multiple people including his cellmates, a psychiatrist, and the sheriff's office. However, Valenzuela was not investigated for or charged with the murders. He was released after serving three years in prison on other charges.

In 1967, Valenzuela was charged with a murder on a federal reservation in Arizona. During an interview with his attorney, Valenzuela again volunteered that he had committed the McKillop/Sterrenberg murders, this time providing more details. Valenzuela subsequently repeated his confession to a defense psychiatrist and to his subsequent attorney in the 1967 murder. Valenzuela eventually was convicted of the federal reservation murder and was sentenced to fifteen years. Valenzuela died on November 8, 1973, after being stabbed during a prison confrontation. None of his confessions about the McKillop/Sterrenberg murders were publicly known at the time.

This alleged confession was made only to Carol. At the time of the confession Carol and Bill were going through a divorce and a bitter custody battle.

In 1974, more than twelve years after the homicides, Carol Macumber, an employee of the MCSO, reported that her husband Bill Macumber told her that he had killed McKillop and Sterrenberg. This alleged confession was made only to Carol. At the time of the confession Carol and Bill were going through a divorce and a bitter custody battle. The MCSO subsequently interviewed Bill, who denied committing the murders. The MCSO obtained a handgun and a set of fingerprints from Bill. The State's experts concluded that a partial latent fingerprint lifted from Sterrenberg's vehicle matched Bill's, and that ejector markings on the shell casings that had been found at the scene matched Bill's handgun.

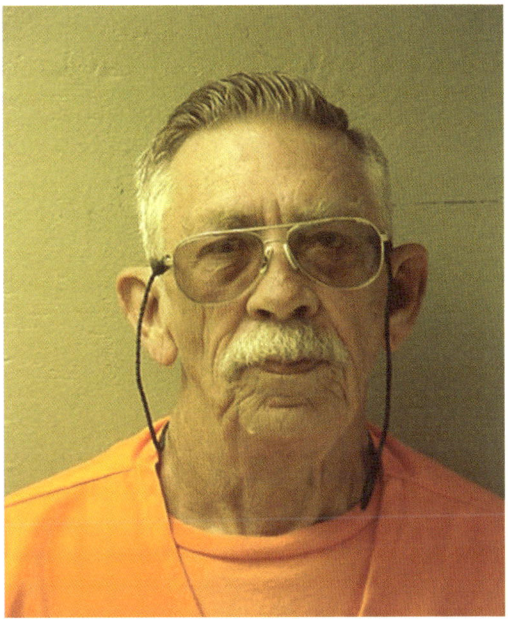

In 1975, Bill was convicted of two counts of first degree murder and sentenced to serve two concurrent terms of life imprisonment. The Arizona Supreme Court reversed the convictions on the ground that the trial court erroneously excluded testimony by a defense expert. At his retrial, the defense, which had not known about Primrose prior to the first trial, called her as a witness, but she recanted the statements she had made in 1962, testifying that she had made up those statements because she was mad at her mother. Despite Valenzuela's multiple confessions, the trial court refused to permit the defense to present evidence regarding them, ruling that they were hearsay. Bill was again convicted and given two life sentences.

The Arizona Justice Project, an organization that helps to overturn and prevent wrongful convictions in the State of Arizona, began work on the Macumber case in 2000. The Justice Project hopes to receive a clemency order from the Governor of Arizona. The Justice Project submitted evidence to the Board of Executive Clemency that casts doubt on the information provided to the state by Carol Macumber, who certainly had a motive to lie due to the impending divorce and custody battle between the couple. The Board issued a unanimous decision to Governor Jan Brewer to grant clemency, but the recommendation was denied in November of 2009. The Justice Project continues to work to obtain freedom for Bill Macumber.

Despite Valenzuela's confessions to a cellmate, his two attorneys, and to a psychiatrist, the trial court refused to permit the defense to present evidence regarding Valenzuela's 1964 and 1967 confessions, ruling that they were hearsay.

Letter / BILL MACUMBER

May 12, 2009

Dear Mr. Hammond, Professor Bartel, Donna, Katy, Sharon, Rich and all other members of the Justice Project,

I fear that because of the high run of emotions Friday I may have failed to properly express my extreme gratitude to all present. If I missed anyone please forgive me. I am so terribly grateful to each and every one of you for your faith, dedication and the extreme effort you have continually shown on my behalf.

The past nine years have taken us beyond that attorney/client relationship. In truth it has bound us together in a common cause. We have become friends and I do not use that term lightly. Friends are and always will be those very special people in your life.

Throughout the past nine years we have shared frustration, a sense of helplessness and too, disappointment. Friday gave each of us reason to set that all behind us. True, what took place at that hearing does not prove my innocence. Still, I saw the faces of the Board members and I listened to their words. Had they been polled as a jury would have been polled, I know beyond all doubt their verdict would have been not guilty. I later found that same thing to be true of those DOC staff members present. That fact alone lifts my heart beyond all possible words.

I know without any questions that we would not be where we are at present without the great presentation made by all of you to the Board. Not only did your works cast considerable doubt as to my guilt but also your absolute belief in my innocence. The Board listened carefully to your words and found them to be utterly convincing. Those five people hear many stories and are not easily swayed. You did a wonderful job and I along with every member of my family thank you from the bottom of our hearts.

I do not know what will happen now but whatever happens cannot change what has taken place to date. I still have been unable to come down from my cloud nine. When I returned to Mohave I found several inmates waiting patiently for me at the gate. When I told them the results of the hearing they couldn't wait to spread the word and I have been shaking hands and receiving pats on the back ever since both from inmates and staff members as well.

In closing let me once again express my deepest thanks to all concerned for what you have done. We have been unable to prove my innocence to the world and perhaps never will. Still, freedom has become a real possibility.

Know this as well. Because of all of you and because of my wonderful family I truly consider myself to be the most fortunate of men.

My Deepest Thanks,
William W. Macumber

"Darkness to Light" / *BILL MACUMBER*

They cast me into a world desolation ruled,
A world where hope was not allowed.
A world littered with shattered dreams,
Dark beneath an ebony cloud.
All of those things I held close and dear
Had been ripped from out my life
Leaving nothing but long and dreadful days
Filled with fear, with tears, with strife.

Suddenly those oppressive clouds did part
And the sun came shining through.
Not from any effort that came from me
But from effort that came from you.
It was you who reached out and took the hand
Of this old and helpless man,
Exiling darkness and beckoning hope
To light this world where I now stand.
Dedicated to all of you very wonderful people who made
the writing of this piece of poetry possible.
"Thank you"

"Thoughts" / *BILL MACUMBER*

To harbor hope rather than despair
To seek rather than to ignore
To help rather than to hinder
To smile rather than to frown
To reach out rather than withdraw
To give rather than to take
To lead rather than to follow
To Be rather than not to be

ROBERT **McCLENDON**

SERVED 17 YEARS OF A LIFE SENTENCE

PLACE OF CRIME
COLUMBUS, OHIO

Courtesy of the Ohio Innocence Project
Researched by Nicole Billec, Whitney Frazier, and Amanda Rieger

On April 25, 1990, a ten year old girl was allegedly abducted from her Columbus, Ohio, backyard. She said that a man grabbed her, pulled her over a fence, tied a sock around her eyes and put her in his car. He drove to a nearby abandoned house, took the girl inside and raped her.

After the assault, the man drove with the girl to a convenience store and went inside. While he was inside, the girl jumped from the car and ran home. She didn't tell her mother about the attack until the next day when her mother noticed that she was acting and walking strangely. The victim then told her mother that Robert McClendon, the victim's biological father, had abducted and assaulted her the previous day.

The victim was taken to a hospital where a rape examination was conducted and doctors confirmed that the girl had been assaulted. When asked in the hospital who had attacked her, the victim said "I think it was my dad, but I may be wrong because my eyes were covered." According to court documents, the victim had only seen McClendon once in her life before the day of the assault.

The victim then told her mother that Robert McClendon, the victim's biological father, had abducted and assaulted her the previous day.

A limited lab test failed to identify the presence of semen on the swabs collected during the exam or on the victim's underwear. No DNA testing was performed.

According to court documents, the victim had only seen McClendon once in her life before the day of the assault.

McClendon was charged with kidnapping and rape in May 1990. While awaiting trial in early 1991, he took a polygraph test on the condition that the results be admitted as evidence in court. A State Highway Patrol examiner found that his answers "could be a deliberate attempt at deception." McClendon waived his right to a jury trial and his bench trial began on August 26, 1991.

The main evidence against McClendon was the testimony of his daughter who identified McClendon as her attacker and the state's allegation that he had failed a polygraph examination. Defense lawyers presented alibi witnesses who said McClendon was driving around with a friend at the time of the crime. On August 28, 1991, McClendon was found guilty of rape and kidnapping. He was sentenced to fifteen years to life in prison.

Robert with his grandchildren

In 2004, McClendon filed for DNA testing on evidence collected from the crime scene. Prosecutors opposed the testing, saying there was no evidence to test because tests in 1990 were negative for semen. McClendon then filed a motion in state court seeking DNA testing, but a Franklin County judge never responded to McClendon's request.

In 2007 and 2008, the Ohio Innocence Project, a component of the Rosenthal Institute for Justice at the University of Cincinnati College of Law that assists the convicted innocent, worked closely with reporters at the *Columbus Dispatch*. The reporters evaluated cases of Ohio defendants who claimed to be wrongfully convicted and who had been denied access to DNA testing in the past.

McClendon's case was one of thirty chosen for representation by the Ohio Innocence Project and pro bono DNA testing by an Ohio lab.

McClendon's case was one of thirty chosen for representation by the Ohio Innocence Project and pro bono DNA testing by an Ohio lab. In response to requests from the Ohio Innocence Project, Franklin County prosecutors searched for the evidence in McClendon's case and found that the rape kit had either been lost or destroyed, but the victim's underwear had been preserved. They agreed to conduct testing in April 2008. Three months later, test results came back showing that another man had committed the assault. McClendon was freed on August 12, 2008, after serving nearly seventeen years in prison for a rape he didn't commit.

"Hello Truth!" / ROBERT McCLENDON

You've been there all the time.
But some people don't want to see you.
Some people don't want to believe you!

Hello Truth!

We fight for you.
We fought because of you.
But there are those who live with the lie.
Those who sleep with the lie!

Hello Truth!

They played hide and seek with you and the proof.
But when surrounded by lies and deceit.
No wonder it took so long to find you!

Hello Truth!

With God's armor you call to dress me.
I knew in time you would bless me!

Hello Truth!

I believe that a lie can take on a life of its own as in my case. But the truth is patient and the truth will catch up and outlast a lie. The truth is like math, it's exact! It is what it is because it is. I wrote Hello Truth when I was waiting for my DNA results to come back. I believe the truth will always come back to bless you if you fight for it hard enough and long enough. Hello Truth!! July 2008

BEVERLY **MONROE**

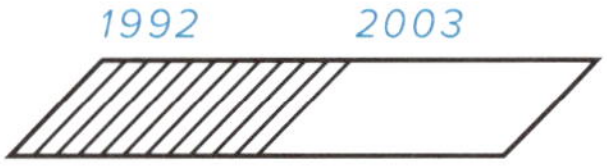

SERVED 11 YEARS OF A 22 YEAR SENTENCE

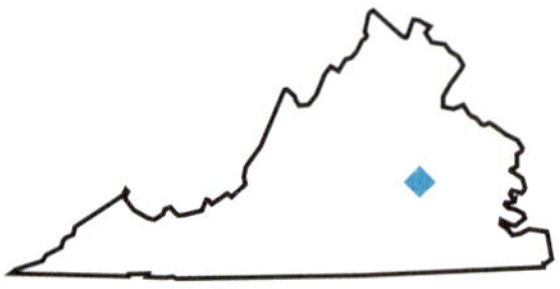

PLACE OF TRIAL
POWHATAN COUNTY, VIRGINIA

Courtesy of the Mid-Atlantic Innocence Project
Researched by Molly CaJacob, Kelvin L. Morris, and Angela Neyer

On the morning of March 5, 1992, wealthy art collector Roger de la Burde, age sixty, was found dead on the couch of his Powhatan County, Virginia, home by his girlfriend, Beverly Monroe. It appeared that he had shot himself in the head with his own gun. The death was initially ruled a suicide and the crime scene was processed as such.

The investigator assigned to the case, David Riley, believed the death was a homicide. Ignoring all other evidence, Riley focused his investigation exclusively on Monroe. He questioned her numerous times, manipulating her in an effort to obtain a confession. He tried to convince Monroe that she had been present at the time of death, but had blocked the memory because of the trauma of the suicide. Monroe repeatedly told the investigator that she was not there and had not fallen asleep after dinner as Riley theorized. After eight hours of interrogation, Riley successfully manipulated Monroe into believing she may have taken part in the crime. Monroe subsequently had a conversation with Riley in which she expressed uncertainty about the events of the day in question. Unbeknownst to her, Riley recorded the conversation.

Riley continued to pressure Monroe, asking her to meet him at a park to discuss the case. Hoping to get a signed confession, Riley gave Monroe an outline of the case against her, offered her a fake plea bargain, and told her that if she was found guilty, she would not be able to see or contact anyone, including her three children. By the end of this meeting, Riley had convinced Monroe to sign a statement that she had fallen asleep and was in the house when the death occurred. After this "confession" was obtained, Monroe was arrested for murdering her boyfriend.

Ignoring all other evidence, Riley focused his investigation exclusively on Monroe.

In November 1992, Monroe went to trial. The Commonwealth of Virginia introduced evidence that, based on the position in which the deceased was found, he could not have shot himself. They also had a witness who claimed that Monroe had tried to buy a gun from her earlier that year. The Commonwealth portrayed Monroe as a jealous girlfriend, angry that her boyfriend was having a child with another woman. Additionally, the Commonwealth presented the "confession" that Riley had Monroe sign. Despite defense evidence showing the death to be a suicide, Monroe was found guilty of first degree murder and use of a firearm in the commission of a felony. She was sentenced to twenty-two years in prison.

Beverly and her grandson Asher

After Monroe was convicted, her daughter, a lawyer who worked for the U.S. Commission on Civil Rights, assembled a team of lawyers to take on her mother's case. Monroe filed for a writ of habeas corpus arguing that the Commonwealth had illegally suppressed evidence, resulting in an unfair trial. Monroe's petition listed more than ten pieces of evidence that the Commonwealth had withheld, including a deal made with the witness who testified Monroe had tried to buy a gun from her in exchange for her testimony; witnesses who had seen a dark car driving away from the decedent's house the night of his death; a statement from the decedent's groundskeeper, who had moved the gun upon finding the body; medical documents ruling the death a suicide; and notes taken by two women who observed her eight-hour interrogation by Riley, which supported Monroe's contention that she had been manipulated and maneuvered by Riley.

The habeas corpus petition was granted by the District Court, and in 2002, that decision was upheld by the United States Court of Appeals for the Fourth Circuit and the United States Supreme Court. In June 2003, Monroe was freed when the prosecutor announced that he would not retry Monroe. Today, Beverly Monroe is spending her time with her three children and her grandson. She has not been compensated for the eleven years she spent in prison.

In June 2003, Monroe was freed when the prosecutor announced that he would not retry Monroe.

"Prison Home" / BEVERLY MONROE

This is a simple drawing of the space in which Beverly lived in prison, as well as another simple drawing of the little home in the country she dreamed of living in while in prison.

"Dream Home" / *BEVERLY MONROE*

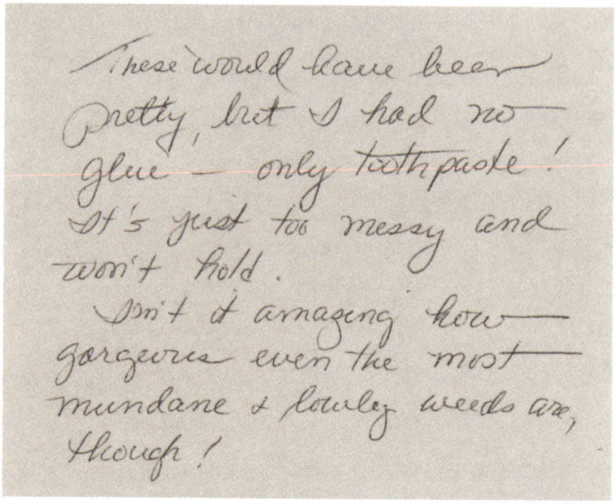
These would have been pretty, but I had no glue — only toothpaste! It's just too messy and won't hold.
Isn't it amazing how gorgeous even the most mundane & lowly weeds are, though!

Cards / *BEVERLY MONROE*

Most of what was represented in prison as "recreation" was not; often the women were put out in the heat for long periods, or the cold. The "yard" was bare, except for patches of dandelions or other little grasses that somehow managed to grow. In spring, in one corner, the most beautiful little wood pansies would come up, with delicate, pale lavender stems.

The wood pansies were the hardest to work with (glue or paste was also "contraband"). Drying them was a rudimentary process and required pressing the petals and leaves carefully between sheets of tissue paper and collecting them in my German dictionary, which I always carried outside with me, both to read and to use as a flower press. (A "contraband," which was a baseless label and merely a way to deny the presence of beauty and its appreciation.)

I seldom got to go outside because of working in the "school" (the business/computer class) from about 7:30 in the morning till about 4 pm. But being out where one could see trees beyond the fence, and sky, and find these bits of natural beauty was restoring, despite the images of uniformed men with rifles in the background, and the raucous noise that was so much a part of the life inside and outside of the walls.

MIKE **PIASKOWSKI**

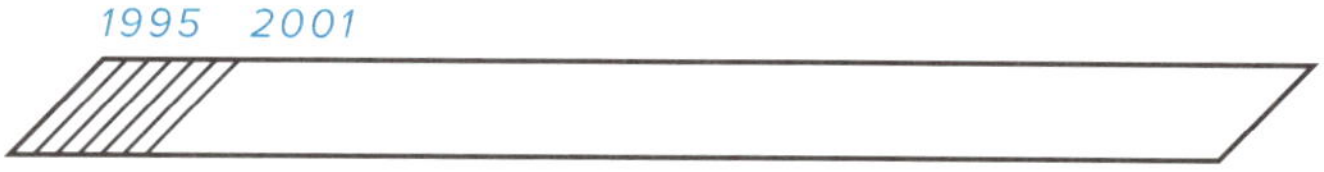

SERVED 6 YEARS OF A LIFE SENTENCE

PLACE OF TRIAL

GREEN BAY, WISCONSIN

Written by Kelvin Morris
Researched by Molly CaJacob and Angela Neyer

On November 22, 1992, Tom Monfils, an employee of the James River Mill in Green Bay, Wisconsin, was found dead at the bottom of a two-story barrel of wood pulp. Attached to his neck was a fifty pound weight. The coroner revealed that he had died of asphyxiation. Prior to his death, Monfils had been attacked by some of his coworkers when they found out he snitched on another union member, Keith Kutska, who had stolen some electrical cord. After the attack Monfils went missing. A search was begun, and his body was discovered the next day.

No charges were immediately filed. For over two years, the Green Bay police investigated the crime until a coworker and friend of Kutska's went to police with Kutska's admission of the attack on Monfils. Through his friend, Kutska identified six coworkers who were allegedly involved in the attack including Mike Piaskowski. At trial, the prosecution presented two witnesses who had heard, but had not seen, what happened the morning of Monfils' death. In October 1995, based on these testimonies, the jury convicted Piaskowski and the other five defendants of first degree intentional homicide and sentenced them to life imprisonment.

After exhausting his direct appeals, Piaskowski petitioned the Federal District Court for a writ of habeas corpus...

After exhausting his direct appeals, Piaskowski petitioned the Federal District Court for a writ of habeas corpus, arguing that the record contained insufficient evidence to sustain his conviction. The United States Court for the Eastern District of Wisconsin granted the writ, and forbade the state from retrying Piaskowski. The State appealed, but the writ was affirmed by the United States Court of Appeals for the Seventh Circuit holding that there was insufficient evidence to support Piaskowski's conviction beyond a reasonable doubt and that retrying him was barred by the double jeopardy clause of the Fifth Amendment. On April 3, 2001, Piaskowski was released from prison.

"Doin' Time" / *MIKE PIASKOWSKI*

PRISON LIFE – DEADLY STRIFE,
den of evil fare.

ATMOSPHERE – BURNS SO CLEAR,
toxin in the air.

ERODED WILLS – WASTED SKILLS,
souls lay vacant bare.

ETERNAL STAYS – ENDLESS DAYS,
abysmal deep despair.

SORDID NEEDS – TWISTED DEEDS,
bitter sad affair.

CAUSTIC BLAME – UGLY SHAME,
guilt for all to share.

SHATTERED DREAMS – NIGHTMARE SCREAMS,
tainted empty prayer.

FAMILY TIES – SIBLING CRIES,
slain in mode unfair.

JUSTICE BLIND – TRUTH UNKIND,
bias far from rare.

FATAL PART – FUTURE DARK,
enough not seem to care.

Imagine this; You are an innocent person in prison, sentenced to 'life' for a heinous crime that you did not commit; You are surrounded by evil and sin, depression and despair, loathing and hatred; with no one willing to recognize or admit the injustice.

In 1999, shortly after my latest appeal had been turned down, and another lost Christmas with family and friends, the emptiness and hopelessness began to take its toll. In an attempt to document these emotions, I put together my first (and only) doggerel poem. It's called "Doin' Time". January 1999

ATIF RAFAY

2004 PRESENT

CURRENTLY SERVING 6 YEARS OF A LIFE SENTENCE WITHOUT THE POSSIBILITY OF PAROLE

PLACE OF TRIAL

SEATTLE, WASHINGTON

Written by Jennifer Miller
Researched by Guy Cardamone and Claire Gutmann

On July 12, 1994, eighteen year old Atif Rafay returned home with his friend, Sebastian Burns, also eighteen, to find his parents, Dr. Tariq and Sultana Rafay, and sister, Basma, murdered in their Bellevue, Washington home. They had been bludgeoned to death with a baseball bat. The walls, floor, and ceiling of Rafay's parents' bedroom were covered in blood, bone, teeth, and tissue. Large amounts of blood were also tracked throughout the property.

Burns called 911 and, fearing the killer might still be in the house, the two waited in the street for police. For the next few days, Rafay and Burns allowed police to test their clothing, interrogate them and search their belongings without exercising their right to counsel. No blood, bone, or tissue were found on either boys' body or clothing. DNA found at the crime scene did not match Rafay or Burns, and evidence showed that at least three people were involved in the killing.

DNA found at the crime scene did not match Rafay or Burns, and evidence showed that at least three people were involved in the killing.

Because both Rafay and Burns were originally from Canada, the Canadian Consulate obtained permission from the Bellevue police to return the boys to Vancouver, Canada. Despite their full cooperation with police and their escorted and legal return to Canada, Rafay and Burns were later deemed prime suspects in the murder case and police labeled them fugitives. Legal counsel for Burns and Rafay recommended they remain in Canada after observing the actions of the Bellevue Police.

A month after the murders, an FBI informant told Bellevue investigators that a Muslim cleric in Seattle had ordered Dr. Rafay killed because of his involvement with the Canadian-Pakistan Friendship Organization and his teachings of the Koran. Police never acted on this tip or any other tips they received after the murders. In 2003, a close friend of Dr. Rafay, and another member of the Canadian-Pakistan Friendship Organization, Riasat Ali Khan, was murdered outside his home in Vancouver. His murder also remains unsolved.

Nine months after the murders, when police failed to uncover any other evidence, they contacted the national police force in Canada to initiate a sting operation to elicit confessions from Burns and Rafay. Posing as violent criminals, undercover police officers engaged in a fifteen week set-up operation in which the officers coerced Burns and Rafay's involvement in staged criminal activities. Although entrapment is illegal in the United States, this practice is legal in Canada.

Photo courtesy of www.rafayburnsappeal.com

Police tapes showed the boys tried to sever their connections with the "criminal group" multiple times, but officers used direct threats of violence, and death, to keep the boys involved. Eventually, Canadian police elicited reluctant confessions of murder from both teenagers, as well as from another friend, Jimmy Myoshi, containing many inconsistencies from the actual crime. The police threatened to charge Myoshi with conspiracy in the murder if he did not implicate Rafay and Burns in the triple homicide. Myoshi signed an indemnity agreement in exchange for his statements.

After serving six years in a maximum security, pre-trial facility in British Columbia, Canada, Rafay and Burns were extradited to the United States to await their trial. They were held in a maximum security jail in Seattle where they spent four years in solitary confinement spending one hour a day out of their 4' x 6' cell before their trial began in November 2003.

Almost ten years after the brutal murder of his family, Rafay and Burns were convicted of three counts of aggravated first-degree murder.

Had the boys' confessions been obtained in the United States in the manner in which they were obtained in Canada, they would not have been admitted into evidence. However, the judge allowed the confessions in while ruling key evidence for the defense out, including the FBI tip linking the murder to Islamic extremism. The trial judge also allowed the undercover Canadian police officers to hold themselves out as experts on how innocent people would respond to the employed tactics while disallowing the defense to put on expert testimony to refute the undercover agents' statements.

Almost ten years after the brutal murder of his family, Rafay and Burns were convicted of three counts of aggravated first-degree murder. They were both sentenced to three consecutive life sentences without the possibility of parole. Burns and Rafay are still in prison and are currently preparing an appeal.

"On the Margins of Freedom" / ATIF RAFAY

Once upon a time, I saw a documentary with black-and-white film footage of Glenn Gould taken soon after his first recording of the *Goldberg Variations*, in which he had taken such extraordinary liberties — excessive liberties, as some would say — with Bach. Although by then in his mid-twenties, on film the pianist gives the impression of being still almost a boy, still very much the prodigy. He is seated outdoors, wrapt against the cold in a muffler, suit and sweater, but sans the usual gloves. At first, Gould answers his interviewer reluctantly, as if unused to conversation. He shifts around in the chair awkwardly, as if unused to furniture. He speaks in quick runs, and punctuates them with abrupt halts. But gradually enthusiasm overcomes diffidence. As he warms to his theme, he becomes himself: voluble, playful, precise. The nimble fingers dance his ideas for the camera; the face radiates happiness and confidence. The words were nothing reticent. "I would like to try my hand at being a prisoner," he said. "I've never understood freedom. To be incarcerated would be a true test of mobility of spirit."

I had known Gould's recordings and writings for over a dozen years when I saw this declaration; but I had been incarcerated almost as long, and I didn't think that I understood freedom. I certainly didn't hope that prison would help me do so. I felt, rather, that it had left me bereft. If I had been changed, it was not for the better. For that matter, I felt glad that Gould himself had not gone on to, as he put it, try his hand at being a prisoner. Although he had retired from the public eye, abandoned the concert stage, and devoted the rest of his life to the studio, not that, nor even so unusual a life as the one he led, can be likened to the incarceration that he seemed ready to dare in that youthful interview.

Perhaps his remarks were offhand, no more than callow bravado from a shy genius. His interviewer did not pursue the matter; the images and the cursory words remain enigmatic. I should have liked to ask Gould what he intended with the elusive phrase "mobility of spirit", and I wonder whether he ever came to feel that he understood freedom. For all the obscurity, one thing, at least, remains vivid in my memory: his powerful sense of something as yet undisclosed to him of freedom while in it, of something elusive but nevertheless essential to attain. With reverent passion and devout curiosity, his words reach at the predicament of the spirit in the toils of the everyday. They are properly philosophical. They make a problem of freedom, so often taken for granted; and perhaps philosophy has no higher calling than to make us aware of what is taken for granted by drawing our attention to this something problematic about life that constitutes its very meaning.

Still, I have reason to mistrust my fascination with what a pianist said a half a century ago. Notwithstanding my admiration for Gould, I have been a prisoner almost half my life, far more than long enough to know that what finds voice here in Gould's words-more than a sentiment, less than an idea-is fairy tale. Is my interest a symptom of the wish to be convinced that incarceration (to the ordinary world an object of revulsion and derision, of horror and contempt) might possess some special worth? That kind of wishful thinking happens all the time in prison, and everyone usually encourages it. Sufferers wish to be reassured that they have had more from their suffering than damage, and so prisoners addle themselves with the hope that their prisons may do more for them than ruin their lives and limit their understanding. Naturally, the world at large finds this only too endearing: their hope obviates the world from doing anything to make the expectation even remotely plausible. Do I, who otherwise scoffs at the substance of things hoped for, merely fasten to Gould's valorization of incarceration with the self-serving fervour with which the poor and meek might cling to Christ's blandishments? If I do not imagine inheriting heaven or earth, am I nevertheless flattered to think that I have tested mobility of spirit, and understood freedom?

I hope not. Even if I thought prison could deliver such understandings, I would have to count it among the sadder bargains imaginable. There are no colder comforts than knowing precisely all that one has missed and that is forever irrecoverable. But I do not harbour even these illusions about what actual incarceration brings; nor can I pretend it offers any illuminations that are not benighted. The proper attitude towards real prisons, these disgustingly efficient contraptions for turning men into ghosts, is the one that Conrad's narrator strikes in *Chance*. Marlow does not ever think to try his hand at prison. It is rather a thing that leaves him sick: "sick and scared."

I do wish I could have an improper attitude. I wish I could talk of trying my hand at prison as if it were an especially enchanting pianoforte; I wish I could belong to the world that can; but I am not so free. I can never think of prison without being sick and scared. This would be a far more orderly essay if it were written in freedom, where I would not feel it necessary to offer an apology for an interest in Gould's imaginings of freedom.

No, it is not because he flatters my predicament that Gould's assertion interests me; I should have found it interesting anywhere. What may seem an objection — that it offers up a paradox, removed from the reality of prison — is precisely what draws me. Gould's words interest me not *despite* their fairy tale quality, but precisely because of it — because they evoke a fairy tale that I loved long before I knew of prisons, and love still, even in dismal rooms and worn-out clothing, after dumb drudgery and cold nights, through solitude and disappointment. I have always loved fairy tales, those of the brothers Grimm and those grimmer than any they told; and the fairy tale that underlies what Gould said that day is perhaps the greatest of them all: the loveliest, and the grimmest.

Its scheme could not be simpler. Once upon a time, there was a soul in bliss. But bliss was lost, and the soul went unrecognised, even to itself. Only in and through tribulation and sorrow, on the wheel of fire at the summit of human experience, was the soul again acknowledged and recovered. The fairy tale tells us that we cannot grasp what we have until it has been lost, that only pain discovers the soul in its perfection. Only through suffering can human beings reach their ultimate potential, only by agony do they become who they are. Though I call it a fairy tale, the narrative forever verges on tragic myth; against the cliff Prometheus is bound and unbound, again and again.

The premise of the fairy tale is the idea of the durable spirit, that old and cherished conviction in the indestructibility of the human soul. This belief in it was powerful enough to ensure that the mediaeval familiarity with the effects of torture is not discernible in the age's representations of hell, in which the victims are imagined to remain lucid. As Erich Auerbach so movingly observes in *Mimesis*, the denizens of Dante's Inferno are not consumed by their ghastly punishments, but become more fully the individuals they are and have been on earth. Their essential character can only be brought into ever higher relief; eternal judgment perfects it. Though each soul is given being by God, its individuality belongs to itself, and is inalterable in essence. These unique souls and their inevitable destinies, which are only figured here on earth, are fulfilled in the afterlife. In such a conception of self, only that which remains constant through carnage counts as real: the soul's mobility is the true measure of its authenticity. So it was that the Inquisition's torturers never feared to destroy those they tormented; for what mattered in their victims was beyond all destruction. God sends souls to suffering and damnation forever, but he thereby preserves them in their human uniqueness forever. They also serve who stand and burn. The blessed and the damned alike find a place that has been prepared to correspond with them and to which they belong absolutely. And by its very irrevocability and infinity of torture, the prison of the Inferno becomes a setting against which the humanity of the damned stands out with a glory that eclipses mere divinity.

It took the Enlightenment to make this formidable story finally incredible, to recognise that human beings are not given to themselves at the moment of their conception nor on the day of their birth, but must be continually made to be: to acknowledge that the process is a construction and not a revelation. Man is *not*, as Rousseau thought, 'born free'; a world is needed to liberate the human spirit. In one way, the idea was far from new. Epictetus had taught it emphatically: "Only the educated are free." But it had been set aside in the era when Augustine could write of the "disease of curiosity" and Lactantius could ask, derisively, what blessing could be had from learning the source of the Nile or any of all that the classical philosophers "raved about."

Only with the renascence of science did humanity begin to be consciously seen once again as something not natural, but artificial: now a product of society and tradition, an existential creation rather than a mystical essence. This perspective anticipated the idea of the foundation of civilisation through repression so controversially diagnosed by Freud. Not for nothing does Hans-Georg Gadamer call *Bildung* — the formation of the self and the attainment of humanity through culture — perhaps the greatest idea of the eighteenth century. The consciousness of freedom is acknowledged to be not immanent in the human species, but something that develops; its progress is the history of the world for Hegel. What had been regarded previously as no more than the refinement of inborn traits is re-imagined in this tradition as becoming human, acquiring an ungiven self, through work upon the self: all that may be subsumed under the rubric of liberal education, education that made free human beings, *liberi*. Liberty thus acquires a new and quite radical sense: no longer is it merely license, or the gratification of essential inner impulses. No longer is it seen as just an absence of constraint. Instead nature itself is seen as potentially a fetter; and autonomy becomes a special power of the human summoned forth by culture tor the realization of authentic freedom. The man of reason is free precisely insofar as he has become sovereign over himself. Having internalised the demands of tradition, and having disciplined himself to maintain control over the dictates of appetite and impulse, the cultured human being is conceived as having both emancipated and mastered himself by the labours of learning, which prove to be the very toils of freedom.

It is only fitting in this context that "toil" should mean *snare* as well as *work*, for it will readily be admitted that this process of becoming free is quite the opposite of freedom as animals —or savages — might understand it. Or our contemporaries, for that matter: if the behaviourist learning theorist BF Skinner felt a need to move "beyond freedom and dignity", it was because in recent years the words so often summon so little. Everything is done to deny the toil of culture necessary to make human beings free in the authentic modern sense, the one founded in autonomy. Freedom becomes a pawn for the politician's prevarication; it plays party to the pornographer's purpose; it promotes the executioner's punishment. The contemporary world continues to live in Dante's imagination, and the same impulse that makes people long for immortality makes them imagine their own inviolability. In this as in so many respects, the Enlightenment has never been universally persuasive even after it became completely convincing. So we reach the idea of prison as a test of the spirit, as in days past earthly life was only a test; and perhaps one of the reasons that many Americans do not shrink from imposing life sentences in prison is that so many of the religious imagine the earth to be merely a prison anyway. Pace Foucault, it is as an irony that we should understand the concurrence of the emergence of the modern prison with the Enlightenment's new consciousness of freedom.

Though his learning was altogether redoubtable in many respects, I do not suspect that Gould was thinking of this history that day. For Gould, prison was an abstraction; he was thinking of his music, the purest of delights, the greatest, the most humanising. He was imagining solitude and piano, scores and recording equipment, a more perfect communion with that hereafter he reached only *in ecstasis*: he was conceiving of his life simplified to the essential activity of his being.

The thought of suffering seems not to have entered into his understanding of prison; it is for him more an emblem of forcible restriction, and therefore of concentration and intensification, under which the truth of freedom might emerge. This idea of prison has not wanted for distinguished proponents. Nietzsche wrote: "One would have to seek the highest type of free man where the greatest resistance is constantly being overcome: five steps from tyranny, near the threshold of the danger of servitude." Before he was incarcerated, Oscar Wilde, ten years his junior, had written: "After all, even in prison a man can be quite free. His soul can be free. His personality can be untroubled. He can be at peace." He would reach a different conclusion in prison.

The thought of suffering would not have been a serious objection to any of them. The aspirational ethic that unites their thinking wilfully embraces pain. The abiding theme of the great tragic fairy tales that Wilde wrote is the transcendental value of agony, on the model of the Passion of Christ. It was, indeed, from Wilde that I first learnt the special poignance of that account of the meaning of suffering, listening to my mother read from The Happy Prince and Other Tales and A House of Pomegranates — though I want to assert it must have spoken to something inside me already, just as I want to imagine it speaks to what is human in us always.

It is, of course, a romantic notion, at once glorious and seductive: perhaps what truly matters in us is proven in a crucible; perhaps what we ought to become we can only attain in extremis. No one emphasised the idea so much, or so eloquently, as Nietzsche:

> *For those human beings in whom I have a stake, I wish suffering, being forsaken, sickness, maltreatment, humiliation — I wish that profound self-contempt, the torture of mistrust of oneself, and the misery of him who is overcome, not remain unknown to them: I have no pity for them because I wish them the only thing which can prove today whether one has worth or not — that one holds out.*

And again: “Only great pain is the ultimate liberator of the spirit ... that long, slow pain in which we are burned with green wood, as it were — pain which takes its time”. Nietzsche and Wilde received what they asked for so far as pain and misery are concerned — not more, though it may seem so, for the excess is essential to agony. Only what goes beyond what can be imagined or thought bearable, what continues when it is no longer endurable, constitutes the true passion of suffering.

So in *De Profundis* Wilde tells us from Reading Gaol — no more talk of “untroubled peace” now — that suffering is not a mystery but a revelation, in which what “one had felt dimly through instinct, about Art, is intellectually and emotionally realised with perfect clearness of vision and absolute intensity of apprehension.” He claims that “sorrow, being the supreme emotion of which man is capable, is at once the type and test of all great Art.” What he does not say is that when he was allowed nothing to read or to write with in Reading, there were no exaltations, neither of sorrow nor of prison; but broken pleas to the warders for books and pen and paper, and warnings of approaching insanity. What he could not know is that after De Profundis was finished, he would come out of prison a broken man and die two years later, never having written more than earnest of anything of importance again. Nietzsche, for his part, had already collapsed in tears in Turin, his arms — if the only too picturesque account is to be believed — around a horse that was being flogged. He never regained lucidity, though his body lived on; and he died the same year as Wilde, in 1900.

Though the world looks askance at abject fates, it is neither as criticisms nor for ironic coda that I mention these cruel culminations; the taste that deplores them confesses its own triviality. In our time Nietzsche is chided for taking things too personally and too seriously; and to some, it seems, Wilde’s death was something of a relief. “Anyone who has read through De Profundis, the long missive he wrote in prison, would not wish for more from his pen”, opines GW Bowersock in The New York Review of Books. I read through it not once but a few times, even before I came to prison; and those who see in it only self-pity miss that, alike in this respect to what Nietzsche wrote, it is written in heart’s blood as few books have ever been. I, for one, cannot find it within me to presume that they knew not what they had won with their long agonies: their wretched and desolate ends stand not as refutations, but as the aptest measure of the value of what they had sought after.

One should not be too hard on the comfortable, however, no matter how hard they have sometimes been on the uncomfortable. The former have, after all, no eyes for what the latter endure and seek to disclose. It is one of the direr dilemmas of suffering that nothing seems so important to communicate and yet is so hopelessly incommunicable. It is this above all that makes sufferers reticent: the conviction that they possess knowledge of a world of experience that others cannot know, nor imagine by any act of will — something before which the garrulousness of pity is profane. Even Dostoevsky, so skilled in depths of anguish, slipped. In the course of writing the serialised novel derived from his time in prison, keenly entitled *The House of the Dead*, he had described, with incredulous indignation, the heedless good humour and cheerful mien of a young parricide who had been in prison a decade. When he received word, before the novel was finished, that the man had in fact been innocent, he was for once at a loss for words: he felt that he could write nothing to enlarge upon such a thing. The fact, he wrote, was too enormous: it spoke for itself.

Nietzsche, I think, would have recognised what Dostoevsky had so uncharacteristically failed to — that "certain ostentatious courage of taste which takes suffering glibly and wards off everything sad and deep." I have personal reasons for finding this minor episode of literary history moving: having lost my own family to murder, and having then been wrongly convicted for it, I hardly ever speak of it, and really I can think of nothing to say that seems adequate. Still, pain isn't strictly proportional to enormity of injustice: though the indignation of being wronged and the frustration of attempts at vindication are excruciating, to be more sinned against than sinning is likely on balance a relief But self-recrimination is misery for the innocent and the guilty alike; the venial errors I have made in my defence teach what stubborn salt regret is to wounds, even without the hangman's metaphysic, as Nietzsche called it, of free will. A friend of mine, before his own suicide, once wished me to die swiftly, and I have no doubt, none whatsoever, of his goodwill.

The world no longer believes in suffering, in the pathos of numinous meaning. That tremendous haut-relief of tragic illumination, which even at a remove calls out for mountains or at least stone for fit monument, has no place in the market economy or the bureaucracy of the modern state. The ecstasy of agony has been recuperated as cliche: everyone has heard — though not from Nietzsche, surely — that what does not kill them makes them stronger; and 'no pain, no gain' is the mantra of fitness buffs and corporate raiders alike. Everyone knows that these formulas are not to be taken seriously: they cover a narrow range of bearable ills, of minor discomforts. We know our lessons in psychology. Harlow's monkeys never recover from their deprivations; they just bury their heads between their knees and scream and scream. So much that is precious is also fragile, and only ashes emerge from some crucibles.

We are no doubt better off without the prisons that tamed Wilde: the metaphysical demands placed on the meaning of suffering have justified too much torture and destruction. But something may be said for the dignity of tragedy once granted to sufferers by the conviction that suffering discloses something worth more than the entire ordinary world. There is another kind of suffering in the prisons of today, quite different from the agony of which Wilde made such profound use. The romance that could survive and indeed thrive in Reading Gaol fares ill in the prefabricated architecture of the modern prison of my acquaintance; these concrete and razor-wire prisons are in their own way less kind to Gould's purpose than even the bricks of Reading Gaol. Outside of the Intensive Management Units — the antiseptic, innocuous name an emblem of technocratic change — the horrors are not so stark, and they emanate less obviously from the power of authority. I doubt I should call them better for being insidious. Gould could content himself by humming Bach Partitas to himself, but he would have found that difficult through the thumps and screeches of death-metal or rap, through yelling and heinous laughter and television. Instead of desolate affliction openly acknowledged and torture murderously inflicted, the better prisons of today put up instead an ugly parody of life, a travesty that leaves no aspect of human existence unsullied. Wilde had no illusions; he knew that he was being deliberately destroyed at the hands of authority. Today, under the rubric of 'corrections' and in the jargon of 'positive programming' — even the .euphemisms are inhuman — the prisoner is enlisted in gainless employment, in banality and triviality, in the perpetual effort at a modicum of physical comfort. Today's prisons are an unending source of the petty thoughts that are among the worst of all human preoccupations. Here there is no crucifixion, but endless Stations of the Way: the steps that must be willingly taken, the knowledge that each volitional step is a movement towards a dismal and mean end, nothing more. As the mediaeval torturers know all too well, the victim's feeling of complicity with the pain can makes the suffering greater. So it is that the knowledge of my own collaboration in the days of my ordinary prison life, in the rituals repeated and the trifling pursuit of utter inconsequence, makes the· awful nullity of the existence worse. Longing, futility, repetition: how uncanny the Greeks were in their psychology of suffering when they imagined the punishments of Sisyphus and Tantalus.

To be incarcerated in the overcrowded prisons of today is to be immersed in a foul-mouthed world pervaded by an underlying bestiality of spirit, a world without ordinary freedom and .no sense of any other. Hell is other people, Sartre reported, and prison is filled with them. The person forced into prison is forced out of the history that made modernity, and plunged instead in the petty stories of pompous thugs with corrupt images and inane slogans inscribed on their bodies like the graffiti on the dirty wall of a dilapidated lavatory. It is certainly true that the pleasure that the mass audience takes in the stereotype of prisoners as monstrous, grotesque predators indicates much more about the mentality of the American public than it does of the reality of the prisoners; but that phantasmagoric image is still closer to epitome than caricature of the prison subculture itself, which is a toxic distillation of the degraded mass culture from which it springs and to which it belongs. The guards fit in as much as the prisoners; for many, the degradation of the prisoners serves to reassure them of the felicity of their shabby and narrow little worlds.

Perversely, it is precisely for the worst that prison is often hardly a punishment. They are in their element. In a few, years of viciousness has made brutishness so deep a habit that when they try a different tack, they lurch awkwardly, carried away by the momentum of prolonged barbarity. Actual violence is almost always honoured in prison in a way, and to an extent, that it never is in civil society. Savagery secures a conscious respect that even the basest mass culture only accords it in the semi-oneiric stupor of a movie theatre; and there is much else in prison life to encourage the overweening vanity so common in prisoners and to comfort the ignorant and dull-witted anywhere. The coarsest racial tribalisms, fundamentalist religions, misogyny, the kitsch cult of sports, committed philistinery, and junk food: all dominate in a hermetic environment that works to make it all seem perfectly natural, as though to induce prisoners and guards alike to forget that anything else exists, could exist, or has ever existed on the face of the earth. Nothing remains uncorrupted: Christianity, which once served to chisel out the most refined human beings in history, here churns out the crude and the coarse, as what inspired *Fear and Trembling* and Bach is reduced to hokum, bestsellers, and banjo songs.

Individual prisoners, of course, may not conform to any of this, but just as an expatriate will unconsciously pick up an accent, so the contagion of prison air is irresistible; and even resilient individuals acknowledge the hegemony in the shy way in which they confess their disapproval of this or that vice, as though embarrassed by their virtue. And so any life that may be led must be one of deliberate and conscientious struggle: an existence of inner exile and alienation, with pantomimes of feigned interest, suppressions of boredom, and expressions of profane pieties. Everything that demands careful development — sensitivity, tact, discernment, incisiveness — dulls in desuetude in prison. Such oddities as curiosity, subtlety, grace, and intelligence, which have little enough place in the world at large, here on noisy days can seem mere fantasies, or at best childhood dreams that cannot quite be recalled. But what the bustle of prison life impresses on me perhaps most terribly is not just frangibility of the soul, but an unlively contempt for what remains: the diminishing expectations, the compromise of aspiration, as each unrecoverable day goes by, accumulating memories that are the stuff of nightmare rather than of myth. I loathe prisoners, of course, but this means I loathe myself, for I am one, damaged and declining, also; and if I hold on to my contempt and self-loathing because they keep me in touch with some iota of what I should still yearn for and might have become in a different, interesting, challenging, various life, I know how ridiculous that nostalgia is. Under these fluorescent lights, quiet repose, whether scholarly, musical, or otherwise, has the cast of desperate escapism and risible *amour propre*. No lover given over to reveries of his beloved, condemned to caress her features in fading photographs, could be less fit than a prisoner to distinguish between liberation and escapism. In this sense is prison apt metaphor for both freedom and determinism — an emblem of their consubstantial uselessness: for prison teaches above all that the future will have no cure for the past, and life no end but the tomb.

To the later Wittgenstein, Gould's claim not to have understood freedom would have seemed a prime example of our capacity to misunderstand language, to make an unnecessary riddle of a problem which is ultimately no more than a question of semantics, a linguistic issue. To understand freedom, he would have argued, means no more than to understand the various uses of the word *freedom* in ordinary discourse. It is a mistake to think that anything especially profound or wondrous strange emerges from clarifying such usage. It is not that languages are games because they are trivial, but because they are conventional. Wittgenstein by no means disputed the existence of genuine mystery: he merely disputed the capacity of language to so much as even approach that mystery. The continuity between early and late Wittgenstein lies most precisely in this basic scepticism for what language could hope to accomplish. The early Wittgenstein thought he could capture the essence of language by reducing it to atomic propositions that gave us pictures of all that is the case in the world, and leaving the rest of human discourse in necessary silence; the later Wittgenstein argued that there is no essence to be captured, but instead a plethora of different language games to be learned. He remained certain throughout, however, that nothing could be written or said that could alleviate the deepest human *Angst* about a world into which our wills penetrate without, however, being therefore able to fulfill our wishes: a world that he found, if not senseless, then one which was at least problematic in its sense. Freedom might perhaps be felt, but never understood. Not incidentally, Wittgenstein was, like Nietzsche, a gifted musician; though this kind of musing seems especially unhelpful when it's noisy.

The hell of other people can reach delirious extremes even in segregation. Perhaps especially in segregation. Bad neighbours are nuisances in ordinary life, but the prisoner in a neighbouring cell is never more than a few feet away, and if he is insane, as is often enough the case, life quickly becomes maniacal. A deranged Vietnam vet (if his ravings may be relied upon) once ranted next door to me in an IMU for weeks on end, before being released directly to the free world. I can only compare this to what I can imagine of the experience of soldiers living underground through artillery bombardment in the Great War; and while their conditions may have been in many respects worse, twisted human syllables are more infuriatingly intrusive than concussive sounds. Another prisoner, Somali Ali (as he called himself), the first neighbour I ever had in the King County Jail, was hardly more than a boy, but already long gone. He took me for a liar when I told him I'd been imprisoned six years already, because his head was filled with tales of the brutality of incarceration inevident on me, and he launched into a practised and deafening tirade — "I'm a mothafuckin' savage, I'm built for this shit" — that went on for days. For lack of practicable options — no earplugs were allowed in the jail — I copied the most striking bits of argot in my notebook, as he interspersed the yelling with crazed laughter. He alternated his beating upon the wall with emissions of scraping sounds that, he assured me, were from the crafting of a shank for the moment when we might come into contact. At one point he tried to pour liquid through a crack in the wall, before I sealed it with toothpaste and newspaper. Eventually he attacked a prisoner who was cutting his hair, and they took him elsewhere. A year later he was shot to death in the prison yard at Walla Walla when he wouldn't end his attack on another prisoner. By sheer coincidence, my attorney at the time had once been his; it transpired that Ali had been brought to America from Somalia for sexual exploitation by an American soldier. He had been shunted through the state's foster system and its juvenile prisons before being graduated to the adult variety. To talk of freedom and spirit is obscene here; the lesson impressed upon me most forcefully, though, is how utterly our ears render us the prisoners of others. The eye's lid has no counterpart in the ear: not even the best earplugs will do for hearing what we do for vision whenever we, mercifully, shut our eyes.

There is perhaps one kind of freedom that prison can make you understand as no other experience. To grasp the indifference of the universe is one thing; to understand the open malevolence of an entire society of human beings is quite another. In the segregation cell you are confronted with the terrible confluence of both. The world is narrowed to a single, dirty room, so dirty that it will never be really clean; and there is no point in cleaning it, since you may soon be moved out of it. But however many times you are moved, the room is always the same: only the din is different. The days are the same as well, and they operate (these artificial days, run by clock rather than sun) on the same, repeated plan. The food comes in on a tray, the tray goes out. I think it was Proudhon who wrote that man is a digestive tube; I remember a character in Proust responding that he hated the man who said it. I can understand the hatred, but I can also understand Proudhon, for in the isolation cell the brief gleam of our lives between dark eternities seems not so much a glimmer as a wan and dingy waste. The self and the spirit, you come to realise, exist not deep within, but extended far beyond you; they have existence only in the connection felt with all that with which you share an interest. In utter desolation all becomes idle, and even if you know you will get out with some life still left to live, even if you think it will be soon, you face an irresistible awareness of the senselessness that life is, alone. Kafka insists that "it's not the money you have earned that you take with you into your grave, but your idle time"; in that sense the solitary cell heaps you with riches for the grave. Even self-mastery, that freedom through culture, can come to seem futile. You may become a stoic if you like, and practise resignation, practise your indifference to all that happens: the system continues on just as before. Hope is irrelevant; only the perpetual loss of the present moment is real, absolute, permanent.

For a long time I would try to live out in as much detail as possible my memory of days long past and far removed: in Pakistan, sunbathed reveries on a warm couch, playing with kittens, a precocious first dinner-date in a Japanese restaurant. But ineluctably the memories came to seem indistinguishable from imagination. Once every connection with your past life falls away, you are left with only your presence in the dirty room. There is one relief: nothing is expected of you, you have no responsibilities, you are at an ultimate and absolute liberty; but it is the liberty of a man immured in an indifferent mausoleum, awaiting his own extinction.

I cannot say that the isolation cell is the only way to even this unhallowed understanding of freedom. As an adolescent I had already formed an idea of its peril, in the condition of error: alone in a room, checking my incorrect mathematics answer again and again, unable to detect any mistake, and yet seeing my error immediately once it was pointed out to me. Without my father to correct me, I thought, I might have forever remained in error. There is, moreover, a moment in Kafka's last novel, *The Castle*, which captures the very emptiness of the quest for freedom taken to its extreme. The protagonist accomplishes his escape from others, only to find himself estranged in his victory:

> *... it seemed to K. as if at last these people had broken off all relations with him, and as if now in reality he were freer than he had ever been, and at liberty to wait in this place, usually forbidden to him, as long as he desired, and had won a freedom such as hardly anybody else had ever succeeded in winning, and as if nobody could dare to touch him or drive him away, or even speak to him; but — this conviction was at least equally strong — as if at the same time there was nothing more hopeless, than this freedom, this waiting, this inviolability.*

I read these words in segregation — with recognition. I laughed. In prison as in no other human affliction is there so fundamental and sustained a rupture of human solidarity, so seamless a sense of enmity.

It is rage rather than freedom that I have come to understand most in prison. I was always much more disposed to laughter than anger and thought fury a brazen confession of moronic monstrosity aat once pompous, ridiculous, contemptible, and mean. But fury is not so alien to me today. I sometimes wonder how the free might feel if they could know what feelings the prisons they have built can inspire in those who are forced to live in them. There is no respite from fury in prison. I now need only think of certain things, and hatred from tiny points engulfs the world. When I think of years spent lying awake from the cold, though there were piles of blankets ready; when I think of the years spent without a note of music, though forced to listen to vulgar conversations yelled from cell to cell in the night, because ear-plugs were not allowed; when I think of the boorish bureaucrats manipulating the mechanisms of misery with their misspelt memos; when I think of the years without dental loss; when I think of the years wasted by the complacent ignorance of jurors and judges, fortified by comfort and imbecile indifference; when I think of all this completely unnecessary cruelty and then of that world that can find it possible to be upset over desserts that do not turn out right at Christmas — then rage unfolds, and it is possible to wish to bring down the world in ruins.

And yet I despise this fury too, because it is finally so petty and useless, so unworthy, so unfree: so much a prisoner's emotion from which there is no escape, so much the very brand of bondage. Nevertheless I feel this abhorrence must not be lost, for it is connected to the admiration of its opposite. To lose it entirely would be to have relinquished all expectations of a possible world governed by living ideas of care and beauty, and animated by the faith that the reach for the sublime, even in prison, perhaps especially in prison, shines still.

I should be the first to concede that the abjection to which jail — a far worse place than prison — reduced me is tremendously funny. All in all, I am glad that I can still find the recollection of that sheer erasure of human dignity so full of mirth, as I discovered in talking of the ordeal one recent morning with another prisoner who had been there at the same time that I was, and for almost as long. From the remove of our very relative, entirely comparative safety, we could laugh, with that terribly energetic hilarity of relief, at the common, indelible memories. Memories of waking long before dawn from hunger pangs, in the purple half-light which glowered all night, only to await like dogs, with inane anticipation, the plastic trays bearing a breakfast consisting of a single egg, a single cup of porridge, three slices of 'brown' bread, a half-pint of milk, and the junk that I never ate — the margarine and packets of sugar and drink flavouring. Of the ravenous, animal hope that the oatmeal would be thick, followed by disappointment when it was as thin as saliva; and of yet how rapidly that disappointment would give way to greedy, animal satisfaction in scraping every drooling iota of gruel off the tray, with gratitude for it being oatmeal and not less nutritious cornmeal, farina, or grits. Of grovelling with just the right mixture of effortful plaintiveness and amicability for an extra leftover sacked lunch consisting of a sliver of entirely unwholesome processed meat between two slices of bread, a tiny bag of pretzels, and a blessed piece of fruit.

Memories of thanking departing prisoners for the foul gift of their used sheets and blankets, which could then be traded in on the weekly sheet exchange so that I might have two with which to ward off the cold. Of frantic desperation in trying to get the attention of the functionary who was sent, after months of prisoners' complaints about the frigid cells in which we shivered, to take the temperature, but who officiously measured it — the face so bland, so serious, so warm — in the toasty hot core of the building where the guards ate take-out and cackled. Of the obese, porcine body and stolid visage of the senior administrator with the ridiculous rank of major, who received without a trace of irony the solicitous words of a judge about the excellence of the facility and the difficulty of his constraints. Of spending the entire hour permitted outside the cell in the shower, to keep warm. Doing it all naturally, complaisantly, as though dignity were something that did not exist.

This may not seem quite entirely funny. The humour may be, to some, a touch elusive. The comedy comes from the droll reversal by which brutality assumes the mantle of righteousness precisely by the victory of its own insensibility, or rather, its imbecile sensibility. It abides in the constant ironic suppression of outrage in an environment in which the irony will never be perceived, and the constant acceptance of unacceptable cruelty that will never be recognised as such because it is what is established — it is the absolute entrenchment of evil among human beings too banal to recognize it as such. I can laugh at all this, until my stomach contorts into iron knots, in much the same way that I laughed uncontrollably one day after the recitation of an impeccably mannered young graduate student teaching sociology, who delivered in her well constructed paragraphs, with the aptest expressions of face, voice, and word as cues of moral disapproval, an account of the plight of the mentally ill in Soviet asylums held in cages and blasted with icy water from hoses as they protested incoherently. The laughter mixed relief at being removed from the futility and suffering, with a sense of power in having the capacity to perceive its abjection. Since I have a far happier conscience laughing at cruelty directed at myself, I find my own memories even funnier — however much I might want to disapprove.

I know now better than I should like my bare requirements for a life recognisably human, perhaps recognisably mine: the seclusion of the single cell, the adequate food, the blessed if imperfect earplugs, the books, papers, and music, the tenuous strands of hope that ravage what they sustain. know that prison is not a space for understanding freedom but a place of creeping corruption. What I love nonetheless in Gould's words is that they sound a tune to which our ears are unaccustomed, one that promises of perfections not yet imaginable, of freedoms as yet unconscious, even if they are not here. Life is problematic; something is missing; ardour is of it.

I am tempted to think that Gould came to comprehend why prison could not have given him the understanding he had sought. The paradox of freedom through toil, in toil, is perhaps never more vivid and yet also more consummately vindicated than in the performance of written music. The pianist is asked to train in sinew and nerve to reproduce with exactitude a score not of his own devising, to maintain fidelity to this text. Yet this feat is achieved not merely when the technical difficulty of the work is no longer an obstacle, but when the score is so absorbed that it belongs completely to the performer. The performer then becomes an interpreter and comes at last to share in the inner texture of the relationship with that ineffable other with which the composer was engaged when composing the work. Just as we do not originate the language we speak, but develop our power of expression by learning it, so learning a piece does not make the pianist merely a slave to the composer. Nor is there a question of struggling *against* the composer to express oneself. Rather, the very chains of the composition become the means for expression and the space of freedom for the imagination.

Gould was the paragon of a creative interpreter, and in the decades after his breakthrough record, his playing changed. His recordings withdrew from willful romantic extravagances without ever ceasing to be personal or poignant. In the essays he wrote to accompany his recordings of the unsurpassable last three piano sonatas of Beethoven — Beethoven, who claimed that music is a higher revelation than all of religion and philosophy — he avoids hyperbole to emphasise instead their subtler charms and quieter satisfactions. Nabokov was impishly fond of puncturing cliches about the opposing cultures of science and art — both, in his view, philistine — by extolling the passion of pure science and the precision of poetry: the best of Gould's recordings annihilate any sense of contradiction. In these interpretations analytic clarity and absolute control become inextricable from and indispensable to originality of expression and imaginative freedom. Nothing is merely wayward; nothing is for effect; he serves the composition and it serves him in a beautiful equipoise.

A quarter century after that first celebrated recording, Gould was moved to record the *Goldberg Variations* again; he could not have known that it would be his final record. In one of his last interviews, he explained his dissatisfaction with what he now considered the faults of his earlier interpretation. "The purpose of art is not the release of a momentary ejection of adrenaline," he finally averred, "but the gradual, lifelong construction of a state of wonder and serenity." A state of wonder and serenity anothing is so far removed from prison's unhallowed halls.

And yet prison is not, after all, without its cruel, special illuminations. Reverence, that rarest of virtues, peeks out from time to time. If the hanged man on the gallows holds the entire world in balance, so does the prisoner have a free view. Sisyphus is of most interest precisely at the moment of leisure, in repose before the toil begins anew. In the rare silent moments of darkness, after the lights go out, when a gleam lights' a page or headphones resound, nowhere so much as in prison do the pejorative connotations of the term *escapism* lose their point — if not, perhaps, all their sting. The work of art is more than luxury or decoration in prison: it can become the substance of life itself. Here, in the very pit of crude fatuity and dull compulsion, those works of human frailty, those arts that were once the privilege of *liberi*, the free, the rich, and the mostly happy, assume an overwhelming and astonishing significance for the wretched, as if their inmost savour and secret, the elusive quality of their perfection, had been hidden away undisclosed, awaiting this only too human need.

I must imagine it some consolation still — only not happily, nor, happily, ever after.

> *This intense conviction of the existence of the self apart from culture is, as culture well knows, its noblest and most generous achievement.*
>
> *–Lionel Trilling*

JULIE **REA**

2002—2004

SERVED 2 YEARS OF A 65 YEAR SENTENCE

PLACE OF TRIAL
LAWRENCEVILLE, ILLINOIS

Courtesy of the Downstate Illinois Innocence Project
Researched by Andrew Cleves, Sean Martz, and Clement Tsao

On October 13, 1997, an intruder brutally stabbed and killed Julie Rea's ten year old son, Joel, in the middle of the night in their Lawrenceville, Illinois home. At the time of the murder, Rea, a Ph.D. student at Indiana University, was home for a visit with her son. The police focused on Rea despite her detailed description of the intruder. Awakened at 4 a.m. by Joel's haunting scream, Rea survived a vicious attack by the man she encountered in Joel's room. Startled by her entry, the murderer dropped the knife and fled.

Although there was no motive or evidence showing that Rea had killed her only child, she was indicted on October 12, 2000 on capital murder charges. Having exhausted her life savings on private counsel, Rea filed a *pro se* petition requesting the appointment of two capital-qualified attorneys to defend her at trial. To prevent her from receiving these attorneys, prosecutors announced that they no longer intended to seek the death penalty. As a result, a public defender without capital case experience defended Rea. He was out-matched by three opposing prosecutors whose only evidence was that she was in the house with her son. The prosecution's theory of the case portrayed Rea as a modern day witch by appealing to the sentiments of the conservative east central Illinois jury. They presented testimony from Rea's ex-husband stating that Rea had considered aborting Joel when she first found out she was pregnant. On March 4, 2002, Rea received a sixty-five year sentence for her son's murder.

In 2002, an ABC program, 20/20, aired Rea's story. The broadcast eventually led to a confession by Tommy Lynn Sells. The Downstate Illinois Innocence Project, an organization that provides assistance to attorneys representing the convicted innocent in downstate Illinois, engaged in an intensive investigation of Rea's case and developed extensive corroboration that Sells was in the area at the time of the murder. Sells told investigators details about the murder that only the killer would know.

> The investigation demonstrated the shoddy, and occasionally dishonest, work done by the Illinois State Police...

In June 2004, the appellate court vacated Rea's conviction based on a legal issue and ordered her immediate release. Despite the overwhelming evidence that Rea was innocent, prosecutors re-arrested her as she was being released from prison. Once again, she was incarcerated in a local county jail awaiting a trial to prove her innocence.

The Downstate Illinois Innocence Project, and the expert defense provided by the Bluhm Legal Clinic at Northwestern University and the Center for Wrongful Convictions conducted an extensive investigation prior to Rea's second trial. The investigation demonstrated the shoddy, and occasionally dishonest, work done by the Illinois State Police and local law enforcement authorities. On July 26, 2006, a jury found Rea not guilty of killing her son in 1997.

Rea moved to Michigan where she dedicates time to work on behalf of wrongfully convicted women across the country.

WISH YOU
WERE HERE

Teatime / *JULIE REA*

If you had asked me what tea time was like twelve years ago I would have told you it was a table set with lace or linen, likely both, some familiar china in various floral attire and whatever biscuits or baked goods and small sandwiches might have been readily available to my mother that day. She'd have cream and sugar out; we always drank an English tea. And one didn't sit down in a hurry or feel a rush while seated. One enjoyed, and was satisfied. Worries weren't welcome, rather words were used to share feelings and news of our days and upcoming events.

Inevitably my mother would share a youthful glee at having her daughter and grandson drop by and say "we're so yucky!" This ritual of an afternoon teatime at grandmothers had become one way of enjoying Joel's quickly passing toddler and elementary years. He had outgrown the slurred and mistaken consonant sounds, so his grandmother would enjoy the memory of him, sometimes by capturing a word or phrase and enjoying it with him later, as a reminder of the earlier moments as well [Hence the 'y' instead of 'l' in what would be 'lucky' but she still joyfully pronounced 'yucky'!].

Joel loved his grands. And he loved grandma's teatime. As much as anything else about the teatime he loved it because of his love of his grands. They loved it, because we were all together when having it. And so he learned to delight in the moments when time stood still and we could enjoy each other and the merry moments that tasted good and were beautiful.

It contained the things that a little boy could most easily love and celebrate loved ones with: a sugary cup of warm tea with milk, or, more honestly, warm milk with tea! The little sandwiches and nibbles were to his liking, and could be dissected at will, played with as he liked, and eaten when they were no longer resistible. It was perhaps a somewhat permissible tea setting to be sure, but it was still a very certain teatime.

It was a place just a step outside of the world's rush and darker cares. Joel relished being where the only expectation was coming together to partake and enjoying being there to share. Perhaps because of the nature of that place, time seemed to hold its breath and hesitate, while we were seated there. And in my memory it is as though these moments are in some ways transient and remain without their cares.

But as the years wore on reality upset that table in the harshest of ways. Into that carefree paradise came a thief and murderer. Joel was taken. His mother left alive, in the middle of the night in their home some few miles from their grandparents' house containing that merry table with all of its memories and pleasures.

For the next 9 years a fight for justice for Joel would be waged. And that fight would include a fight for his mother as well. I was wrongfully prosecuted. Convicted. Sentenced to 65 years in prison. And then after serving three of those, released to be retried – and finally exonerated. The man who killed Joel is now on death row, in TX, having gone on to kill other children, before he was caught.

In prison I learned many things. One was that there was no civility to be found there. Only in the memory and love that family and friends held for me were my hope. In a place where routine becomes a monotonous monster devouring your identity and sanity I found a few ways to maintain the spontaneity of my spirit and keep my soul alive. One of the ways was to hold close —when I could get it—a cup of tea.

It wasn't made with water boiled at 208 degrees, or steeped at 175 degrees for a minute, exactly, so that it didn't get bitter. There was no choice of green, white, or black. No china, or glass to drink from. I used the same plastic cup that was my bowl, glass, cup, mug, and plate. It was made with water from the leaky facet at whatever temperature was the hottest I could get from the hot water knob at the moment. And it was the generic tea that came in the only box I could get from commissary as an inmate, if I had money on the books to order something. I had no sugar or milk for it. But did have some honey packets and was thankful for that when I could get it.

And I found that, even with all of the divergences — and believe me, everything except the tiny little leaves inside the bag, was different — just to have that cup of tea was a truly transformative experience. It was a cup of grace in a semi-clean chewed up ugly and otherwise undesirable plastic cup. It was a bit of heaven in the midst of hell.

It was hope. It was love and happiness, a sip away. It held memories of all my people and the good times we had together. Reminding me again that they were still holding me close even though I couldn't feel them with my skin. It was a way of connecting to everything that was right in my life. The good reasons I had to go on, and keep believing, and keep fighting for the truth all came alive in each eloquent wash of flavor as I took in another bit of the life restoring drink.

One of the few fortunate wrongfully convicted people in America I am now free. But I continue to be very aware that many others are not. This is not a problem that has been solved. And for each innocent person we lock up we leave a guilty one free to roam the streets and commit more crimes. In my case the man went on to kill and rape at least three more children before being caught. And that is a very conservative estimate. I now write a woman whom I know to be innocent. Jeannette will often relate that in her day the one solace and kindness she has found has been a peaceful — savored — cup of lukewarm tea. She is — as I was — surviving the best she can. She is sustained with the only civility she can find in a truly uncivil place.

Now when I have tea, as I do daily, I not only enjoy thoughts of Joel, I also think of those who may be sipping from chipped and scarred plastic, their weak and lukewarm tea, trying to find in it the will to go on as they fight for their very lives. Teatime has become more for me than just a pleasure, it has become a symbol of the spirit's struggle to survive.

KALVIN MICHAEL **SMITH**

1997 PRESENT

CURRENTLY SERVING 13 YEARS
OF A 28 YEAR SENTENCE

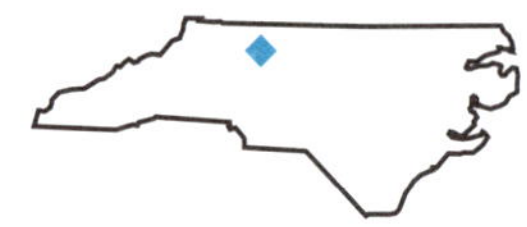

PLACE OF TRIAL
WINSTON-SALEM, NORTH CAROLINA

Written by Kelvin Morris
Researched by Molly CaJacob and Angela Neyer

On December 9, 1995, in Winston-Salem, North Carolina, thirty-three year old Jill Marker was brutally beaten while working at the Silk Plant Forrest, an artificial plant store. She was struck in the head twenty times with a blunt object. Two customers heard moans coming from the back of the store and they discovered Marker in a pool of blood. Marker survived the attack, but suffered permanent brain damage and is now blind. She is unable to care independently for herself or her son whom she was pregnant with at the time of the attack.

The initial investigation led police to Kenneth Lamoureux. Lamoureux had recently been released from the psychiatric ward of the local hospital after his wife had him committed for trying to kill her. Police believed that Lamoureux knew Marker from her former place of employment, a childcare center attended by Lamoureux's children. Marker had told friends that Lamoureux would stop by the store when she was working, but would never buy anything. On the night of the attack, two women spotted Lamoureux in the store. They later identified him in a police lineup. Investigators pursued Lamoureux, searching his apartment and car, and testing his DNA. Nothing linked him to the murder. The only DNA recovered at the crime scene belonged to Marker.

Almost eight months after the attack, investigators focused their attention on Kalvin Michael Smith. A caller to the Crime Stoppers tip line gave Smith's name as the assailant in the attack, but investigators did not question him until he was brought in on a warrant for an unrelated charge. The caller was an estranged girlfriend who was mad at Smith for dating someone else. Smith agreed to take a lie detector test to prove he was not involved in the crime, which he passed. When Marker was able to communicate by nodding her head, she conveyed to investigators that her attacker was a black male even though she could not remember anything else, including her pregnancy or the night of the attack. Investigators again focused on Smith when a different girlfriend who was also angry with Smith for cheating told police that he confessed to her that he was Marker's attacker.

Smith agreed to take a lie detector test to prove he was not involved in the crime, which he passed.

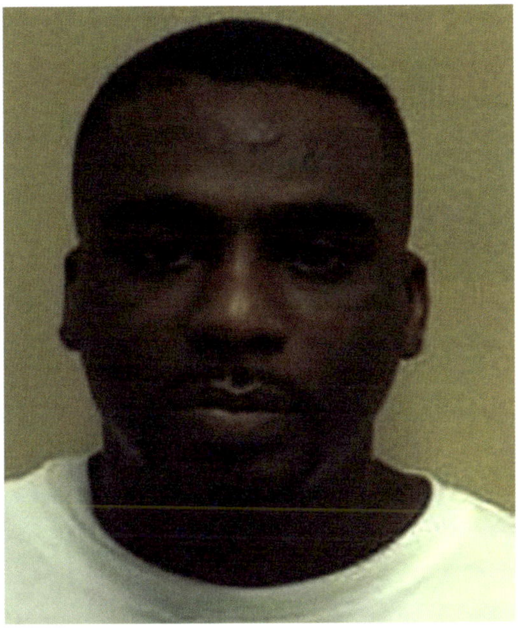

Investigators brought both Smith and the girlfriend in for questioning. They threatened to make the girlfriend an accessory to murder if Smith did not confess. Smith signed a statement claiming he was at the store with a friend in order to rob it. A friend of Smith's corroborated his confession although he gave inconsistent statements to police. It was later found out that prosecutors had threatened Smith's friend with prosecution if he failed to fully cooperate.

Almost two years after Marker's attack, on December 5, 2007, Smith was convicted of assault with intent to kill and was sentenced to twenty-eight years.

Almost two years after Marker's attack, on December 5, 2007, Smith was convicted of assault with intent to kill and was sentenced to twenty-eight years. In 2003, the Duke Law Innocence Project, a volunteer student organization that works to exonerate victims of wrongful convictions, took his case. Most recently, the Innocence Project requested a new trial. They argued on Smith's behalf that prosecutors relied on false testimony to get a conviction, withheld a videotaped police interview of Marker failing to identify Smith while identifying a white male suspect, and ineffective counsel. A superior court judge denied the request. Smith can further appeal to the North Carolina Court of Appeals, and if necessary, to the North Carolina Supreme Court. Smith remains incarcerated.

"Wrongfully Convicted in North Carolina" / *KALVIN MICHAEL SMITH*

My name is Kalvin Michael Smith and my life made a tragic turn Dec 5th 1997. That was the day I was wrongfully convicted in Winston-Salem, North Carolina. Words cannot express at all, the feeling of being incarcerated for a crime I did not commit. Being wrongfully convicted is like being buried alive and screaming at the top of your lungs for help, but no one can hear you. My family and my children have also had to suffer because of my wrongful conviction. I don't think I will ever have faith in the judicial system again in my life. I'll always remember that the same system I looked for justice from, was the same system that served this injustice upon me.

I also find it sickening that while all the evidence points to my innocence, the Attorney General and the District Attorney are fighting with all they have to uphold my wrongful conviction. Nobody should ever be imprisoned for a crime they did not commit and no amount of money can bring back the many years I have lost due to this injustice.

My family members are passing away right in front of my eyes and I've missed watching my children grow. Pain is now my middle name and I'll forever be scarred. Wrongful convictions must come to an end all across the world. There is no justice for the victims when the guilty go free and the innocent suffer. Most people don't care about wrongful convictions, but they fail to realize that injustice don't discriminate and can come knocking on anybody's door...

WRONGFULLY CONVICTED IN NORTH CAROLINA...

My name is Kalvin Michael Smith and my life made a tragic turn Dec 5th 1997. That was the day I was wrongfully convicted in Winston-Salem, North Carolina. Words cannot express at all, the feeling of being incarcerated for a crime I did not commit. Being wrongfully convicted is like being buried alive and screaming at the top of your lungs for help, but noone can hear you. My family and my children have also had to suffer because of my wrongful conviction. I don't think I will ever have faith in the judicial system again in my life. I'll always remember that the same system I looked for justice from, was the same system that served this injustice upon me.

I also find it sickening that while all the evidence points to my innocence, the Attorney General and the District Attorney are fighting with all they have to uphold my wronful conviction. Nobody should ever be imprisoned for a crime they did not commit and no amount of money can bring back the many years I have lost due to this injustice.

My family members are passing away right in front of my eyes and I've missed watching my children grow. Pain is now my middle name and I'll forever be scarred. Wrongful convictions must come to an end all across the world. There is no justice for victims when the guilty go free and the innocent suffer. Most people don't care about wronful convictions, but they feil to realize that injustice **don't** discriminate and can come knocking on (Anybodys) door..

Kalvin Michael Smith

NANCY **SMITH**

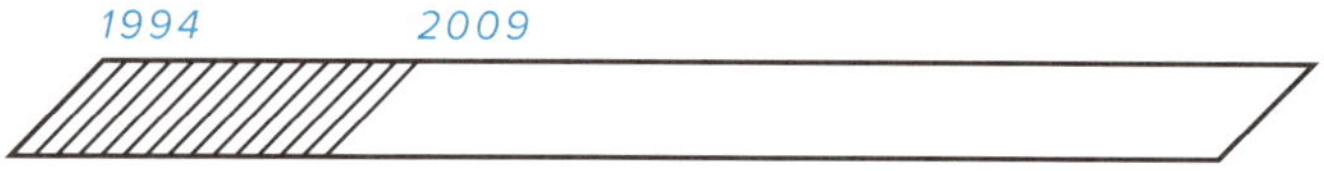

SERVED 14.5 YEARS OF A 30 TO 90 YEAR SENTENCE

PLACE OF TRIAL

LORAIN COUNTY, OHIO

Researched by Kamiikia Alexander, Jessica Lantaff, and Kayla Delk

In May 1993, a four year old girl claimed that a man named Joseph sexually abused her with a stick. The girl claimed that Nancy Smith, a bus driver for the Lorain County Head Start program and mother of four, drove her and her classmates to Smith's home where the abuse occurred. The girl's mother reported the alleged sexual abuse to the police. Smith was investigated concerning the allegations, but after Smith passed a lie detector test, and with several inconsistencies in the girl's story, the investigation was concluded.

Unsatisfied with the results of the investigation, the girl's mother unleashed a public media campaign by openly criticizing the police department and launching grievances with the mayor. The investigation was suddenly re-opened and many more children came forward with stories of abuse. These stories were inconsistent with some children claiming their attacker was a black man while others claimed he was white.

Police came into contact with Joseph Allen, a retired sanitation worker, when he went to the police station to report a stolen vehicle. Allen fit the description of the dark-skinned attacker. He had also been convicted of sexual battery of a child in 1985. Police put Allen in a line-up, but nine out of ten children failed to identify him as their attacker. The children's stories also differed on where the attacks occurred. Some children claimed the abuse occurred at Smith's home, others claimed it occurred at Allen's home. Head Start records indicated that Smith had never been late in transporting the children to the program, leaving her no time to deviate from her bus route.

On August 4, 1994, Smith was sentenced to thirty to ninety years in the Ohio Reformatory for Women in Marysville, Ohio.

At trial, the videos showing the children's inconsistent statements were excluded as evidence. After only six hours of deliberation, the jury convicted Allen and Smith of gross sexual imposition, rape, attempted rape, and complicity to rape. On August 4, 1994, Smith was sentenced to thirty to ninety years in the Ohio Reformatory for Women in Marysville, Ohio. Allen received five life sentences. The parents of four of the children were awarded millions of dollars in their civil suits against the Head Start program.

Nancy and her children

On appeal, Smith's convictions were upheld and she was also denied post-conviction relief. In 2004, the Ohio Innocence Project (OIP), a component of the Rosenthal Institute for Justice at the University of Cincinnati College of Law that seeks to assist the convicted innocent, began working on Smith's case. In 2009, Smith's lawyers filed a motion for resentencing on Smith's behalf arguing that the court never entered a final, appealable order as the sentencing entry failed to show how Smith was found guilty—by guilty plea, jury, or by the court—as is required by law. The Lorain Common Pleas Court agreed and after extensively reviewing the record, including a brief by the OIP outlining all of the evidence of innocence, the court also ruled that the evidence was insufficient to uphold Smith's convictions. On June 24, 2009, after spending fifteen years in prison the judge then acquitted both Smith and Allen.

...after extensively reviewing the record, the court also ruled that the evidence was insufficient to uphold Smith's convictions.

"Freedom" / NANCY SMITH

Inspired by Michelangelo's ***The Hands of God and Man***

This is very hard for me to sit and write what I need to say, why, who knows. This painting represents the one person who was with me on a daily basis. GOD. In those sad and lonely days, when I didn't feel like no one cared, He was just a finger tip away. When your life has been turned upside down for something you did not do is so devastating, that you just don't know where to turn. It took me 14 and a half years to realize that I was never alone, that God was always just a finger tip away, all I had to do was continue to reach out and he would be there as he always was. Out of all the things that I could of painted, this is was what was truly my strength in that dark and lonely place. The support and love of my family has also been a big part of my journey, and I will also be so ever grateful to them for their love and support, and for my daughter Amber who never stopped trying to bring me home. Her determination and God's love have brought home, finally after 14 years. To anyone who reads this please just never give up, always have faith, because God is just a finger tip away. And if you let Him, He will take you by the hand and lead you, to wherever you need to be. I thank my children Adam, Amber, Courtney, and Chase for loving me and staying strong also with the injustice not only to myself, but also to them.

They were the reason that I got up everyday.

RAYMOND **TOWLER**

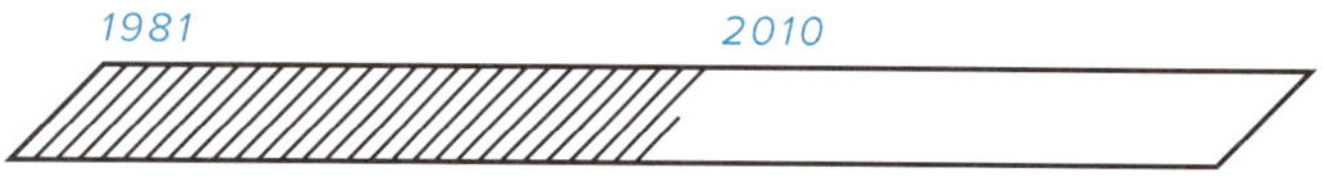

SERVED 28.5 YEARS OF A LIFE SENTENCE

PLACE OF TRIAL
CLEVELAND, OHIO

Courtesy of the Ohio Innocence Project
Researched by Nicole Billec, Joseph Lehnert, and Amanda Rieger

On May 24, 1981, an eleven year old girl and her twelve year old male cousin were walking in a park in Cleveland, Ohio, when a man who claimed an injured deer needed their help lured them into a wooded area. The man pulled out a gun and assaulted the boy, forcing him to lie on the ground while he raped and sexually assaulted the young girl.

Towler resembled the composite sketch of the rapist...

Near the same park, roughly three weeks after the crime, a park ranger stopped Raymond Towler for running a stop sign. Towler resembled the composite sketch of the rapist, created with the help of one of the victims, and the park ranger brought Towler into the police station where he was photographed. Several days later, both victims chose Towler from a photo array, although the identification took the boy nearly ten minutes and the girl nearly fifteen minutes. Two other witnesses also chose Towler's photo from an array. Based on these identifications, Towler was charged with rape, assault, and kidnapping.

At Towler's trial, the two victims testified that Towler attacked them in the park. Both witnesses from the park also testified and identified Towler. One of the witnesses testified that she saw the perpetrator three times on the bike trail the day of the crime. The witness further claimed that he was alone the first two times and accompanied by the victims on the third occasion. The other witness testified that he saw the perpetrator alone and passed by him on the trail.

The only physical evidence presented at trial came from a forensic analyst who had microscopically examined a hair found on the victim. He testified that the hair appeared to be a "negro" pubic hair. The female victim was white. According to the analyst, the hair did not possess a sufficient number of unique individual characteristics to be linked to Towler.

During the trial, Towler testified on his own behalf. He stated that he did not commit the crimes and presented an alibi that he was at home when the crimes occurred. Several witnesses corroborated his alibi.

Photo taken by Ryan Kurtz for *Cincinnati Magazine*

More than twenty years after Towler was convicted, Ohio enacted a law allowing DNA testing in very limited circumstances. Towler immediately filed an application for DNA testing. His request was granted in 2004. At that time, Towler was represented by appointed counsel, and the Ohio Innocence Project (OIP), a component of the Rosenthal Institute for Justice at the University of Cincinnati College of Law that seeks to assist the convicted innocent, was brought on to consult in the DNA testing process. Shortly thereafter, prosecutors were asked to send the pubic hair from the crime scene to the lab. The envelope arrived at the lab empty. One month later, prosecutors said they were mailing material from under the victim's fingernails to the lab. Again the envelope arrived empty. Eventually, some clothing worn by the victims was sent to the lab. No semen was found on the clothing and testing ended.

In 2008, the *Columbus Dispatch* in a joint project with the OIP, featured 30 Ohio prisoners who were seeking DNA testing to prove their innocence. Towler's case was included. The Ohio Innocence Project, now representing Towler, requested additional DNA testing on the clothing even though it had previously tested negative for semen. The clothing was tested using a new technology, Y-STR testing, which isolates male DNA by focusing on the Y chromosome.

More than twenty years after Towler was convicted, Ohio enacted a law allowing DNA testing in very limited circumstances.

In May 2010, Towler received the fourth and final round of DNA results. The Y-STR results from the girl's underwear excluded Towler as the perpetrator finally clearing him after more than twenty-eight years in prison. Days later, Towler was a free man. He was twenty-four years old when he was convicted, and fifty-two on the day of his release.

"Blue Man with the Flag" / RAYMOND TOWLER

The man in the painting is blue, like B.B King plays the blues, because of what the criminal justice system has done to his life. But he holds the American flag because even though he has been cheated by the criminal justice system, he is still a patriot at heart and proud of his country.

"Passing Time" / RAYMOND TOWLER

The 80s were not a hopeful decade at all for me, and I painted Passing Time during this low point in my life. A life sentence with a lawyer who sucked (God rest his soul), and no pleasant or clear future to see. Time seemed to melt away and disappear, just like the clocks in this painting. My life looked as though it would also melt away into the cracks of society's bottomless pit, which is what prison is for those without help.

"Witch Doctor" / RAYMOND TOWLER

The painting of an old black skinned woman represents the long history of the belief in a higher power "God." The practices may change but the strong faith is the same over countless generations. From Africa to Cleveland, Ohio USA.

SHERMAN TOWNSEND

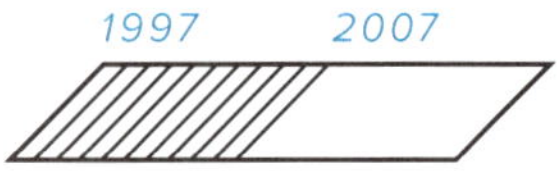

SERVED 10 YEARS OF A 20 YEAR SENTENCE

PLACE OF TRIAL

ST. LOUIS, MISSOURI

Written by Lourdes Perrino
Researched by Zach El-Sawaf and Dominique Mix

On the night of August 10, 1997, Sherman Townsend went to Dinkytown, a neighborhood in Minneapolis, Minnesota, to visit some friends. A burglary had taken place in the same area that night and the woman whose house had been burglarized described the culprit as being a heavy-set black man. Police sent out the description of the suspect over the scanner. Soon after, Townsend, an ex-con who had prior burglary convictions on his record, was picked up and brought to the victim's house. The victim could not positively identify Townsend as the burglar, but a neighbor of hers, David Jones—the real burglar, claimed that he saw Townsend running out of the home, knocking Jones over as Jones was coming home from a bar. Townsend was arrested and charged with first degree burglary.

The victim could not positively identify Townsend as the burglar, but a neighbor of hers, David Jones—the real burglar, claimed that he saw Townsend running out of the home...

As Townsend's trial drew near, prosecutors offered him a plea bargain in which he would serve only four years for pleading guilty to the crime, otherwise he would face twenty years in prison. Confident that he would be found innocent, Townsend rejected the plea deal. At a pre-trial hearing, Jones testified that Townsend was not the man he saw the night of the burglary, but during Townsend's trial, Jones identified Townsend as the perpetrator. After three days of testimony, the jury convicted Townsend of first degree burglary. Due to his prior convictions, Townsend received the maximum sentence of twenty years and was sent to Moose Lake prison. Townsend filed an appeal of his conviction arguing ineffective assistance of counsel at trial, but the appeals court upheld the ruling.

In 2002, the Innocence Project of Minnesota took Townsend's case, but their appeals were also unsuccessful until Townsend saw Jones in Moose Lake prison. Jones had been incarcerated for criminal sexual conduct. He confessed to Townsend that he was the one who actually committed the burglary. Jones said that he was willing to testify that he had perjured himself at trial because the five year statute of limitations for burglary had passed and he wanted to help Townsend clear his name.

Empowered with Jones' recantation, Townsend's attorneys submitted Jones' affidavit confessing to the burglary and revealing details about the crime scene that would only be known by the perpetrator. After receiving the confession, prosecutors agreed to strike a deal with Townsend—his sentence would be commuted to the ten years already served and Townsend would walk out a free man in exchange for him not pursuing a retrial or suing the county. Townsend wanted to prove his innocence, but he also had other concerns, such as his eighty-seven year old mother who had recently suffered several strokes.

He was able to spend five months with his mother before she passed away.

Townsend decided to take the deal, and on October 7, 2007, at the age of fifty-seven, he walked out of prison a free man although the crime he did not commit remains on his record. He was able to spend five months with his mother before she passed away. Today, Townsend lives in St. Paul, Minnesota, where he sings in an R&B band and works as a janitor at the local community center in order to support his son's biweekly kidney dialysis treatments.

"Rhapsody in Color" / SHERMAN TOWNSEND

The title I have given the two Macaws is "Rhapsody in Color." I have a fascination with the color red. I'll try to sneak red into any piece I create. The Macaws gave me a chance to go red mad and gave me an opportunity to experiment with colors in both a pastel and acrylic medium. My sights tend to be drawn to compositions that are colorful while emotionally stirring or sensitive. Both of my pieces were done while I was in prison (2006-2007) and in a mode of hopefulness and looking to the future in a positive frame of mind. Both pieces exhibit the progress I was making in learning to use different mediums and exhibit more of my sensitive side, a place I've come to like.

"Beholding Beauty" / SHERMAN TOWNSEND

The title I've given my bluebird is "Beholding Beauty." This piece is done in acrylic and it was the colors of the bird that got my attention. It would come out even more colorful were I doing that painting today because I wouldn't be as reserved in experimenting with color as I was back then. It was one of my first acrylic pieces and I learned a lot from doing it. To me, the bird was just beautiful to behold and it gave me an opportunity to learn how to make an object the focus of the piece while giving the background less focus; muting it. This was a piece that I couldn't sneak my red in on.

PART III / THE INNOCENTS: HEADSHOTS BY **TARYN SIMON**

CHARLES IRVIN FAIN

Scene of the crime, the Snake River, Melba, Idaho

Served 18 years of a Death sentence

for Murder, Rape and Kidnapping

2002

▲ "© 2003/2010 Taryn Simon. Courtesy Gagosian Gallery."

In her project titled, *The Innocents, artist Taryn Simon documents the stories of individuals who served time in prison for violent crimes they did not commit. At issue is the question of photography's function as a credible eyewitness and arbiter of justice.*

The primary cause of wrongful conviction is mistaken identification. A victim or eyewitness identifies a suspected perpetrator through law enforcement's use of photographs and lineups. This procedure relies on the assumption of precise visual memory. But, through exposure to composite sketches, mugshots, Polaroids, and lineups, eyewitness memory can change. In the history of these cases, photography offered the criminal justice system a tool that transformed innocent citizens into criminals. Photographs assisted officers in obtaining eyewitness identifications and aided prosecutors in securing convictions.

Simon photographed these men at sites that had particular significance to their illegitimate conviction: the scene of misidentification, the scene of arrest, the scene of the crime or the scene of the alibi. All of these locations hold contradictory meanings for the subjects. The scene of arrest marks the starting point of a reality based in fiction. The scene of the crime is at once arbitrary and crucial: this place, to which they have never been, changed their lives forever. In these photographs Simon confronts photography's ability to blur truth and fiction-an ambiguity that can have severe, even lethal consequences.

– Taryn Simon

The following headshots are on the book cover of a larger work, including environmental portraits of the wrongfully convicted, titled The Innocents. All photographs and interviews are by Taryn Simon.

WARITH HABIB ABDAL

SERVED 17 YEARS OF A 20-TO-LIFE SENTENCE

BUFFALO, NEW YORK

In May 1982, a young woman was raped in a nature preserve in Buffalo, New York. Warith Habib Abdal, then Vincent Jenkins, was picked up more than four months after the crime occurred and presented to the victim in a one-on-one showup procedure.

The victim failed to identify Abdal, even though the police told her that Abdal was their key suspect. She then viewed an old photograph of Abdal, returned to the showup, and finally identified him as her attacker. Despite this suggestive identification procedure, despite significant differences between the victim's initial description of the suspect and Abdal, and despite alibi testimony corroborated by work records, Abdal was convicted of rape in 1983. Ten years later, Abdal obtained an early form of DNA testing that yielded inconclusive results. (The test lacked the power to discriminate between more than one contributor of sperm, and the victim claimed she had had consensual sex prior to the rape.) In 1999, hoping that new DNA techniques would work, Abdal's lawyers sent slides and swabs to a private laboratory. The evidence was lost by an overnight mail service. Miraculously, DNA extract from the 1993 testing was found, even though that laboratory had ceased performing forensic testing. Testing of the 1993 extract revealed two male contributors. Abdal was excluded as the source of either profile. Based on this new evidence, Abdal was exonerated and released in September 1999.

Testing of the 1993 extract revealed two male contributors. Abdal was excluded as the source of either profile. Based on this new evidence, Abdal was exonerated and released in September 1999.

"They say I'm the one that's crazy. Ain't that deep? United Snakes, I mean States of America. 'Scuse me, my teeth are loose. They kicked them out in Attica when I was busted for rape. My understanding of the five points of the star: an officer grabbed this leg, one grabbed this leg, one grabbed this arm, another grabbed this arm, and the fifth one stepped between my legs and kicked me in my groin until I bled from the mouth. And the tax dollar paid for that. Didn't you know that? I did seventeen years and they want to give me a dollar and a half and take seventy-five cents of that. All I've asked out of this madness is for three graveyards. One in Clinton, where they murdered my brother, one in Sing Sing, and one in Attica. So when they finish killing brothers in the penal system, at least they can be buried as Muslims.... United Snakes of America is not at war with terrorists. 'Cause if she were, she'd kill the terrorists in this country first. And that's the Ku Klux Klan—my terrorists. Anybody leaving this country—going to another country, talking about fighting the terrorists—you better think twice. Because the war that was before this, the men that lost it, they're in the penitentiary. My evidence is in the penitentiary."

–Warith Habib Abdal

A.B. BUTLER

SERVED 16.5 YEARS OF A 99-YEAR SENTENCE

TYLER, TEXAS

In May 1983, a young woman in Tyler, Texas, was abducted from a parking lot, driven to a rural area, and raped twice.

The victim later identified A.B. Butler from a photographic lineup, a live lineup, and then in court. Butler gave an alibi—he was at a club with friends—that witnesses corroborated. Nevertheless, he was convicted later that year of aggravated kidnapping, with rape as the aggravating factor. Butler continued to push for testing of the biological evidence in order to prove his innocence, but his appeals were denied.

The detective said, "You must be guilty."

Sixteen years later, Butler finally secured access to the evidence for DNA testing. The first round of testing did not yield conclusive results, but subsequent testing on swabs from the rape kit excluded Butler as a possible contributor. The final round of testing confirmed that Butler was not the source of semen found on the victim's shirt. Based on these results, A.B. Butler was freed from prison in January 2000 and was officially pardoned in May 2000.

"When they arrested me and read my Miranda rights, I requested an attorney. The detective walked in the room I was waiting at, and asked me, 'What did I want with an attorney?'... I didn't say anything. He said, 'You must be guilty.' That sprung me right there. I got aggravated. I said, 'I'm not guilty.' He said, 'Why you need a lawyer? It might be two or three days before a lawyer can come here. You say you haven't done this. There's no way she can pick you out. If you go ahead and get through with this you'll be out of here.' With that trickery I signed the waiver of attorney. I had a job interview and other business that needed to be taken care of that day. It was a lot of pressure on me to sign that waiver. When I got into the lineup I was picked out by the victim."

–A.B. Butler

CLYDE CHARLES

SERVED 17 YEARS OF A LIFE SENTENCE

TERREBONNE, LOUISIANA

In March 1981, a Louisiana woman in need of automobile assistance was attacked on the side of the road.

The assailant dragged her from the road, beat her with a pipe, and raped her. Later, a policeman picked up the woman and took her to the hospital. The same officer had seen Clyde Charles hitchhiking an hour before the crime occurred and had ordered him off the road. The police picked up Charles and brought him to the hospital, where the victim identified him in a one-on-one showup procedure. At trial, the prosecution presented forensic evidence consisting of two head hairs found on Charles' shirt and semen found in the rape kit. The victim testified that the perpetrator had called himself Clyde. During questioning about a jacket the perpetrator had left behind, Charles' statement, "Was it blue?" was offered as an admission. The defense argued that the cross-racial identification was mistaken, and that Charles had been on his way home from a construction job he worked with his brother, Marlo, who left earlier, walking down the same road. The jury convicted Charles of aggravated rape in 1982, but he continued to maintain his innocence. For ten years, he unsuccessfully sought a DNA test in state court. He finally obtained testing from a federal court seventeen years after his conviction. He was exonerated and released in December 1999. In April 2000, Charles's brother Marlo was arrested for the same crime, and based on the DNA test results, was subsequently convicted.

Charles's brother Marlo was arrested for the same crime, and based on the DNA test results, was subsequently convicted.

"That was one of the coldest days of my life. Ten women and two men: all white jury. I didn't even have a ghost of a chance running through hell with gasoline trunks on.... I don't care who did it. My brother could have done it. Anyone could have done it. It doesn't make no difference—I don't want to go to prison for nobody. The D.A. told me he didn't care if Santa Claus did it, he was going to convict me for it. I said, 'Well, partner, we got a fight on our hands.' After the trial, the girl's father came over to me and he shook my hand. He said, 'For one poor black man, you put up one hell of a fight.' And I looked at him and said, 'Mister, I did not rape your daughter.' He just lightly eased on away. And I looked at my mommy and daddy and said, 'He thinks the fight is over with; the fight's just begun.' "

–Clyde Charles

CHARLES IRVIN FAIN

SERVED 18 YEARS OF A DEATH SENTENCE

NAMPA, IDAHO

In 1982, a young girl was abducted while walking to school in Nampa, Idaho.

Her body was found days later in a ditch near the Snake River. Police focused their investigation on Charles Fain, who was new to the area. Many men, including Fain, were asked to provide hair samples to be tested against hairs found on the victim. Based on hair comparisons performed by the FBI, Fain was convicted of kidnapping, rape, and murder, and sentenced to death in 1983. Prosecutors also relied on testimony from two jailhouse snitches who claimed that Fain had confessed and provided detailed information about the crime. Fain maintained his innocence, claiming that he was at his father's house in Oregon on the day of the crime. Eighteen years later, Fain secured access to the evidence, and the hairs were subjected to mitochondrial DNA testing. He was excluded as the contributor of the hairs, and the court ordered his release in August 2001. Fain became the eleventh person freed from death row due to postconviction DNA testing.

Fain became the eleventh person freed from death row due to postconviction DNA testing.

"They took me back to a room. Lieutenant Patrick was there and he had a death warrant. He read it, cracked a few jokes, and that was about it.... They had to give us a copy of the procedure. We read it to see how it went. They strap you on the gurney. The spiritual advisor leaves. Then they put the needles in and walk behind this thing and start pushing some buttons. Wouldn't take more than about four minutes."

–Charles Irvin Fain

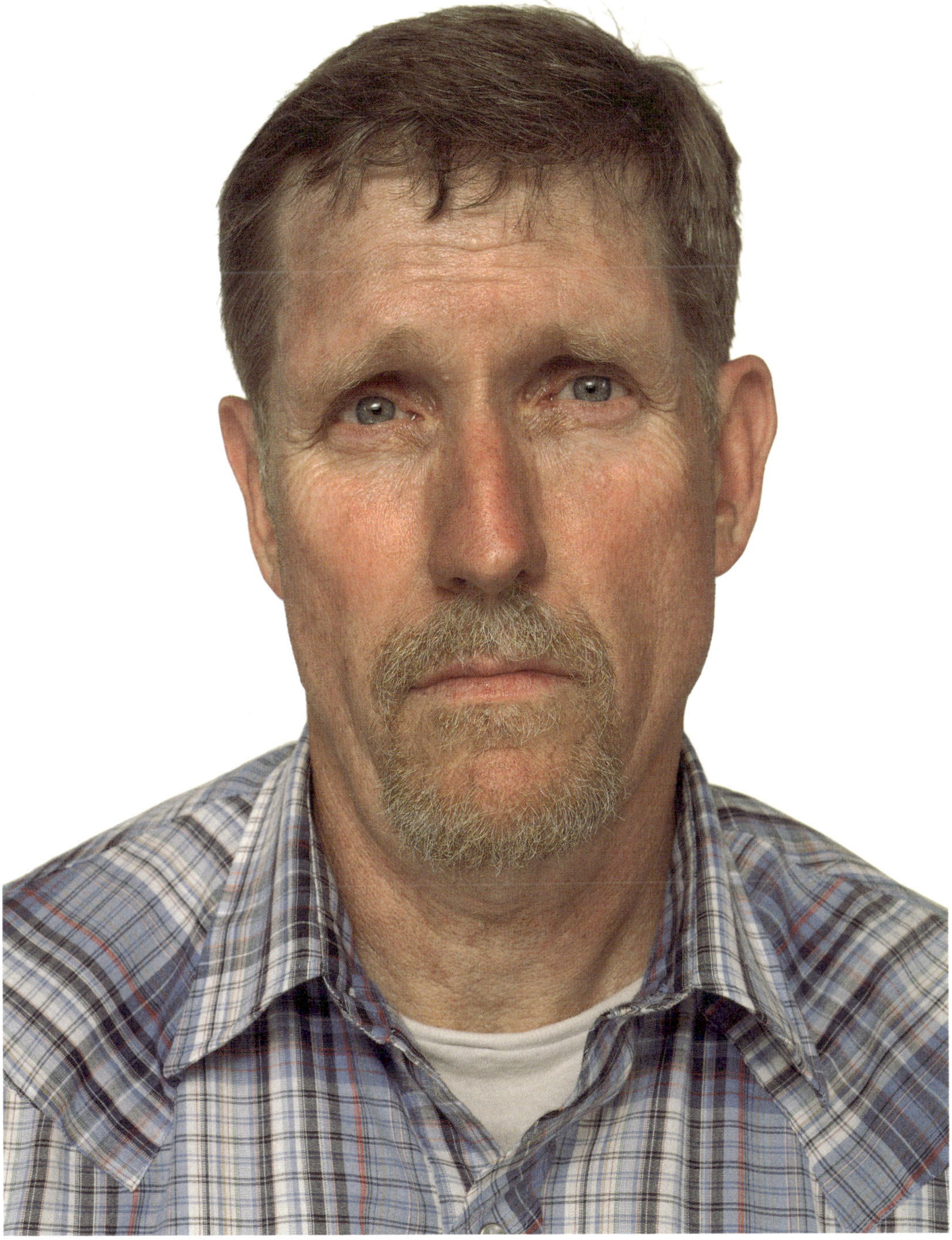

PAULA **GRAY**

SERVED 6 YEARS OF A 50-YEAR SENTENCE

CHICAGO, ILLINOIS

In 1978, Paula Gray, then seventeen years old, confessed falsely to a crime she did not commit, as well as implicated four men who had nothing to do with the crime. Those men became known as the Ford Heights Four—two of them ending up on death row.

Gray, borderline mentally retarded, was questioned about the abduction and murder of a young white couple whose bodies were found in an abandoned house in the Ford Heights section of Chicago. She was

"They took away my family. I hurt so bad on the inside."

interrogated by police in motels over the period of two days before testifying that she was present when the crimes were committed and implicating the four men who would become her co-defendants. Gray recanted her testimony and was charged and convicted, along with three of the four men, of murder, rape, and perjury. Lacking evidence against Verneal Jimerson, prosecutors approached Gray and released her from prison in exchange for testimony against Jimerson. Gray's four co-defendants were exonerated and released from prison in 1996. Gray's conviction was not overturned until 2001. Although prosecutors appealed the decision, Gray was granted a gubernatorial pardon in November 2002.

"They took away my family. I hurt so bad on the inside. I just don't trust no police. I got a gun pointed to my head. They took me to the scene of the crime. There was a lot of blood on the floor and I have not been right since then. I go home, I look under the bed, I look in my closet. What happened to us is wrong. I can't get this out of my mind. I feel like all the guys hate me for confessing. I don't want them to hate me. I love them. I just go through so much."

–Paula Gray

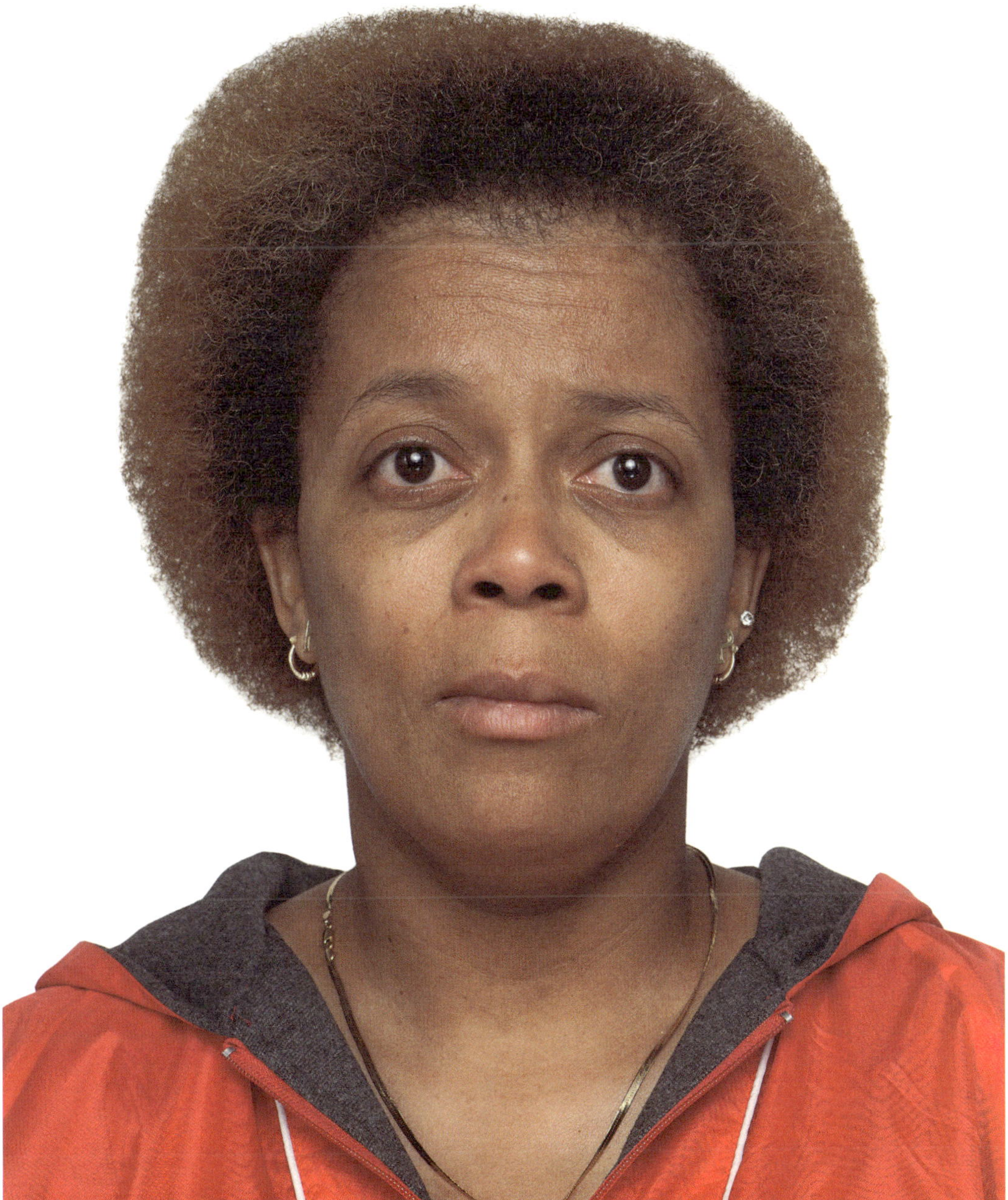

WILLIAM GREGORY

SERVED 7 YEARS OF A 70-YEAR SENTENCE

LOUISVILLE, KENTUCKY

In 1992, two women who lived in the same apartment complex in Louisville, Kentucky, were attacked in their homes. The first victim, twenty years old at the time, was awakened by a naked black man, who used the victim's panty hose to cover his head. The panty hose were removed in the struggle, and the perpetrator fled.

The victim picked someone other than William Gregory from a photo lineup, describing an assailant ten years younger, heavier, and without facial hair. However, after seeing Gregory, a Sears electronics salesman, in the same apartment complex (the only black resident),

> Gregory maintained his innocence and provided alibis for both crimes, but was convicted of rape, attempted rape, and two counts of burglary in 1993.

she later identified him as her assailant. The police inspected Gregory's body for scratches and searched his apartment, but they found no evidence. The second victim, over seventy years old at the time, was assaulted while Gregory was out on bond. Although she also did not pick out Gregory in a photo lineup, she identified him in a one-on-one showup procedure conducted weeks after the crime. Gregory maintained his innocence and provided alibis for both crimes, but was convicted of rape, attempted rape, and two counts of burglary in 1993. After his appeals failed, Gregory sought DNA testing on the hairs left behind in the panty hose. These hairs were determined to be African- American hairs, and were tied to him at trial. As the victim claimed to have had no black visitors in her home, these hairs were presented as necessarily the assailant's. Mitochondrial DNA testing proved that they were not from William Gregory. Gregory was released in 2000, becoming the first person in Kentucky to be exonerated due to postconviction DNA testing.

"The jury's prejudices were in the closet, but the door was cracked. You could tell the door was cracked by the expressions on their faces when my white fiancée said my nails was beautiful and I was handsome. The jury was like, 'What is wrong with her?' They cracked the door so to speak. You could see the prejudice on their faces. The spotters in my case looked at the jury, came back and said, 'He's convicted.' They said that because of what they saw when my fiancée got on the witness stand—she was a very classy white woman, well kept, came from a rich family. They convicted me with their prejudices, their biases. They basically got rid of their pencils and stopped taking notes."

–William Gregory

RONALD JONES

SERVED 8 YEARS OF A DEATH SENTENCE

CHICAGO, ILLINOIS

On March 10, 1985, a twenty-eight-year-old woman who went out late at night to look for a Harold's Chicken restaurant was found raped and stabbed to death in an abandoned building on Chicago's South Side. Later that year, police produced a confession signed by Ronald Jones after a twelve-hour interrogation. At the time, Jones was an alcoholic and living in abandoned buildings.

According to the confession, Jones had sex with the victim and then subdued her after she attacked him. Jones said that the confession was the product of

In 1997, PCR-based DNA testing was used by order of the Illinois Supreme Court, and the results excluded Jones as the perpetrator.

police coercion which included physical assault. Based on the confession, Jones was convicted of rape and murder and sent to death row. Initial DNA testing on the semen recovered from the victim was deemed inconclusive. In 1994, Jones requested that the trial judge authorize DNA testing with newer methods, but the request was denied. In 1997, PCR-based DNA testing was used by order of the Illinois Supreme Court, and the results excluded Jones as the perpetrator. His conviction was vacated in July 1997, and Jones was granted a new trial. Jones remained incarcerated until May 1999, when, after reinvestigating the matter, prosecutors officially announced that the charges were dropped. Jones was subsequently pardoned on the grounds of innocence.

"They wouldn't even ask for the death penalty for O.J. But why was that? Because O.J. had money, he was a celebrity. But me? I couldn't even afford an attorney. O.J. had lawyers people dream about having. Me? If a public defender wouldn't have been free, I wouldn't have even had that. You're not gonna see no rich people on death row, very few of them even go to jail. I have not—to date—seen a rich man go to death row.... It's two types of justice: there's a poor man's justice and a rich man's justice.... I was poor and still is. I'll never be able to feel free. Because as long as I'm poor, the same thing that they did to me in 1985, they can do it to me again."

–Ronald Jones

LARRY **MAYES**

SERVED 18.5 YEARS OF AN 80-YEAR SENTENCE

HAMMOND, INDIANA

In October 1980, two assailants entered a gas station in Hammond, Indiana,threatened the clerk with a gun, demanded money, and then forced her to leave with them.

The victim was beaten with the gun and raped by both assailants before being released. Based on her description and identification, Larry Mayes was convicted of rape, robbery, and unlawful deviate conduct in 1982. According to the description, one of the perpetrators was much taller and heavier than the other. Although they both raped her, only the smaller perpetrator ejaculated. The victim identified Mayes as the smaller assailant in a photographic array, but only after failing to identify him in two live lineup procedures. At some point in this process, without the knowledge of prosecutors or defense lawyers, the victim was hypnotized. None of the fingerprints collected from the scene belonged to Mayes. Serological testing was performed on semen found on the vaginal swabs and underwear collected from the victim, but the results were not useful for identification. After conviction, Mayes fought to obtain access to the biological evidence for DNA testing. For years, the evidence was said to be lost. In August 2000, however, a court clerk was able to confirm that the rape kit still existed and was in the court's possession. DNA testing in 2001 conclusively established that Larry Mayes was innocent, as he had claimed since his arrest. He was exonerated and freed in December 2001.

None of the fingerprints collected from the scene belonged to Mayes.

"Why? Because I'm young, gifted and black. It's always been that way. Even before you was born. I was there. I know. What it really is, is genocide: getting rid of all the young black men so we can't produce. Put 'em all in the penitentiary. There's so many guys in there that are innocent but can't get a chance. They take us, put us in cages, and leave us there. You go there. The whole cell house is nothing but black dudes. It'll always be that way."

–Larry Mayes

ANTHONY ROBINSON

SERVED 10 YEARS OF A 27-YEAR SENTENCE

HOUSTON, TEXAS

In 1986, a young woman at the University of Houston was raped.

She described her assailant as a black man with a mustache wearing a plaid shirt. Based on this description, police stopped Anthony Robinson as he was picking up a car for a friend from a university parking lot. Though he was wearing a plaid shirt, Robinson did not have a mustache and was clean-shaven. Still, minutes later, the victim identified him as the assailant in a one-on-one showup procedure. The prosecution relied mainly on the victim's cross-racial identification, and Robinson was

The prosecution relied mainly on the victim's cross-racial identification...

convicted of sexual assault in 1987. Robinson pressed for forensic testing to prove his innocence, even offering to give police blood samples. He was paroled in 1997 and continued his efforts to prove his innocence. Once he had raised enough money, he sought DNA testing on the biological evidence collected from the victim. Test results proved that he could not have been the perpetrator. After the prosecution's tests confirmed the exculpatory results, Robinson's record was cleared. He was issued a pardon in 2000.

"Since the incident occurred, I've taken on the affectation of making sure I'm presentable when I go somewhere. It's kind of stifling for me 'cause I'm really a casual guy. But if you don't dress up in such a manner as to say, 'Okay, I'm a normal person,' the opportunity is there for them to say whatever they want: 'He fits the description.' Very rarely is somebody going to say: 'He was wearing a shirt, a tie, a pair of slacks, and some hard-soled shoes.' That's not the description that they're going to use to grab you.... I keep records and tabs on where I was, what I was doing, and how long I was there. It's a small price to pay for my freedom. I keep general notations, little scraps of papers.

If I go to the store, I'll keep a receipt or I'll make notations on my calendar. I just recently stopped keeping a logbook—so that's an improvement. My fear is if I stop, it might happen again.... Don't take this the wrong way, but it's kind of hard for a black man to live in Texas and not believe in God. That's the only way you can make rational sense of the irrational things that are happening around you."

–Anthony Robinson

CALVIN WASHINGTON

SERVED 13 YEARS OF A LIFE SENTENCE

WACO, TEXAS

In March 1986, the body of a Waco, Texas woman was found in her home. She had been beaten, strangled, and raped.

Calvin Washington was arrested for the murder based on the theory that he, alone or acting in concert with Joe Sidney Williams, killed the victim in the course of a robbery and sexual assault. Prosecutors presented evidence that the two defendants were in possession of property that belonged to the victim. Witnesses also testified that Washington had made inculpatory statements regarding the burglary. From Washington's home, police seized a shirt that had blood on it, supposedly the victim's. As a result, Washington was convicted of capital murder in 1987. DNA tests proved that the blood on Washington's shirt did not belong to the victim. Testing on semen evidence also proved that neither Washington nor his codefendant had raped the victim. Based on these exculpatory test results, Calvin Washington was pardoned in October 2001. The DNA profile from the rape kit inculpated another suspect named Bennie Carroll, who had committed suicide. Carroll had previously admitted to raping and beating one of the victim's neighbors.

...after leaving jail, I found out my mom was dead. She'd been dead for about two years. No one told me.

"When I got to Highway 6, after leaving jail, I found out my mom was dead. She'd been dead for about two years. No one told me. They said they couldn't get in contact with me. But they knew where I was. It bothers me. I think about it all the time. I go visit her grave. I kept writing her, but nobody ever wrote me back or told me nothing. I found out when I got out. At first, I thought the letters weren't getting out. None of them came back. Somebody had to be throwing them out. She never wrote me back. And then, when I got out, they told me she was dead."

–Calvin Washington

WACO

RON WILLIAMSON

SERVED 11 YEARS OF A DEATH SENTENCE

ADA, OKLAHOMA

In 1982, a young woman employed as a barmaid at the Coachlight Club in Ada, Oklahoma left work late one evening and was found dead the next morning, raped and strangled. Six years later, Ron Williamson, a former minor league baseball player in the Kansas City Royals system, and his friend Dennis Fritz were arrested and convicted of the crime.

Williamson, who suffered from mental illness, was convicted on the testimony of jailhouse snitches, a confession that he had had a dream about the crime, and microscopic hair comparisons linking him and Fritz to seventeen head and pubic hairs found on and under the body. Glenn Gore, the star witness for the prosecution, said Williamson was in the Coachlight bothering the barmaid on the night of the murder. Twenty-three other people in the Coachlight, many of whom had known Williamson for years, had not seen him. Williamson was represented by a blind lawyer who lacked adequate assistance and did nothing about the fact that his client was actively psychotic at the time of the trial. Williamson came within five days of execution. He spent much of his time on death row without proper medication, screaming that he was innocent and banging his head against the cell door. After his conviction was vacated by a federal court on the grounds that his lawyer was ineffective, DNA testing was performed in 1999 demonstrating that neither Fritz nor Williamson was the source of the seventeen head and pubic hairs found on the victim or the semen recovered from inside her. On April 22, 1999, Williamson was released from the same courthouse where he had been convicted. On that day, after it was disclosed that DNA results from the semen matched Glenn Gore, Gore escaped from a work-release program where he was serving time. Glenn Gore was eventually captured and has been charged with the woman's murder.

On April 22, 1999, Williamson was released from the same courthouse where he had been convicted.

"I hope I go to neither heaven nor hell. I wish that at the time of my death that I could go to sleep and never wake up and never have a bad dream. Eternal rest, like you've seen on some tombstones, that's what I hope for. Because I don't want to go through the Judgment. I don't want anybody judging me again.... I asked myself what was the reason for my birth when I was on death row, if I was going to have to go through all that. What was even the reason for my birth? I almost cursed my mother and dad—it was so bad—for putting me on this earth. If I had it all to do over again, I wouldn't be born."

–Ron Williamson

REFERENCES

PART ONE / RESURRECTED

PART TWO / EXPRESSIONS OF THE WRONGFULLY CONVICTED

Barnes, Steven
The Innocence Project, *Steven Barnes,*
http://www.innocentproject.org/Content/Steven_Barnes.php (last visited Nov. 27, 2010).

Brooks, Levon
Radley Balko, *The Bite-Marks Men: Mississippi's Criminal Forensics Disaster,* SLATE MAG., at Jurisprudence, Feb. 20, 2008, *available at* http://www.slate.com/id/2184798.
John Mott Coffey, *DNA Evidence Set Clear Two Noxubee County Men Convicted of Rape and Murder,* http://truthinjustice.org/kennedy-brewer2.htm (last visited Nov. 27, 2010).
Shaila Dewan, *New Suspect is Arrested in Two Miss. Killings,* N.Y. TIMES LATE EDITION, Feb. 8, 2008, at A11.
Levon Brooks Exonerated in Mississippi, Forensic Reforms Underway, Innocence Project Blog, http://www.innocenceproject.org/Content/Levon_Brooks_is_exonerated_in_Mississippi.php (March 13, 2008, 14:05 EST).
Press Release, Innocence Project, Two Innocent Men Cleared Today in Separate Murder Cases in Miss., 15 Years After Wrongful Convictions (Feb. 15, 2008), *available at* http://www.innocenceproject.org (follow the "News & Resources" hyperlink; then follow "Press Releases" hyperlink).
Sid Salter, *State Must Make New Crime Lab, DNA Facility Priority,* LEADER CALL (Laurel, Mississippi), September 19, 2010, *available at* http://leadercall.com/columns/x176920313/State-must-make-new-Crime-Lab-DNA-facility-priority.

Burton, Darryl
Centurion Ministries, http://www.centurionministries.org (last visited Nov. 27, 2010).
Jeffrey Dazey and Washburn University School of Law, *Darryl Burton Talks About 'Life After Exoneration,'* Dec. 15, 2009, *available at* http://washburnlaw.edu/news/2009/2009-12burton.php.
Chad Garrison, *Darryl Burton: Wrongfully Convicted Ex-Prisoner Sues St. Louis, Police Board,* RIVERFRONT TIMES BLOGS (Sept. 1, 2010, 2:28PM), http://blogs.riverfronttimes.com/dailyrft/2010/09/darryl_burton_st_louis_lawsuit.php.
Midwestern Innocence Project, *Darryl Burton,* http://themip.org (follow the "Know the Cases" hyperlink; then follow the "Darryl Burton" hyperlink) (last visited Nov. 27, 2010).

Burton, Darryl *continued*
Nadia Pflaum, *Miracle Man: Darryl Burton Forgives St. Louis. He Just Doesn't Trust It,* RIVERFRONT TIMES (St. Louis, Missouri), Sept. 23, 2009, available at http://www.riverfronttimes.com/2009-09-23/news/miracle-man-darryl-burton-forgives-st-louis-doesnt-trust-it/.

Bush, Keith
Information on file with Adele Bernhard, Pace Law School Post-Conviction Project.
Keith Bush, 17, Charged in Death of Cherese Watson, 14, in N. Bellport, L.I., Information Bank Abstracts, N.Y. TIMES, January 16, 1975, at P38, C1.
People v. Bush, 77 A.D.2d 884 (N.Y. App. Div. 1980).

Cleveland, Alfred
Cleveland v. Bradshaw, No. 1:10-cv-00148 (N.D. Ohio filed Aug. 9, 2010).

Conover, Chris
The Mid-Atlantic Innocence Project, *Chris Conover,* http://www.exonerate.org/case-profiles/chris-conover/ (last visited Nov. 27, 2010).
State v. Conover, 312 Md. 33 (Md. 1998).

Dail, Dwayne Allen
The Innocence Project, *Dwayne Allen Dail,* http://www.innocenceproject.org/Content/Dwayne_Allen_Dail.php (last visited Nov. 27, 2010).

Drinkard, Gary
Michelle Cerulli, *Pair Shares Death Row Stories after Being Freed,* STAR NEWS, (Wilmington, North Carolina), June 23, 2010 available at http://www.starnewsonline.com/article/20100623/ARTICLES/100629862?p=2&tc=pg (last visited Nov. 27, 2010).
Ex parte Drinkard, 777 So. 2d 295, 297 (Ala. 2000).
Northwestern Law Bluhm Legal Clinic Center on Wrongful Convictions, *Gary Wayne Drinkard,* http://www.law.northwestern.edu/wrongfulconvictions/exonerations/alDrinkardSummary.html (last visited Nov. 27, 2010).
Witness To Innocence, *Gary Drinkard,* http://www.witnesstoinnocence.org/view_stories.php?Gary-Drinkard-15 (last visited Nov. 27, 2010).
Wrongly Convicted Database Record, *Gary Drinkard,* http://forejustice.org/db/Drinkard--Gary.html (last visited Nov. 27, 2010).

Elkins, Clarence
Deborah Rieselman, *Wrongfully Imprisoned Man Thanks UC Students for Freedoms,* UC MAGAZINE (February, 2006), *available at* www.magazine.uc.edu/exclusives/elkins.htm.
Dave Sereno, *Killer's Family Hopes for Sentence Reversal or New Trial,* THE REPOSITORY (Canton, Ohio) June 23, 2002, *available at* http://www.corpus-delicti.com/rep_062302.html.
Ohio Innocence Project, *Clarence Elkins—Exonerated 2005,* http://www.law.uc.edu/institutes-centers/ohio-innocence-project/significant-cases/clarence-elkins (last visited Nov. 27, 2010).

Elkins, Clarence *continued*

Phil Trexler, *Young Witness Recants Testimony that Uncle Guilty of Murder, Rape 4 Years Ago,* THE BEACON JOURNAL (Akron, Ohio), *available at* www.truthinjustice.org/elkins.htm (last visited Nov. 27, 2010).

Gillispie, R. Dean

Petition for Post-Conviction Relief, on file with the Ohio Innocence Project.
State v. Gillispie, 2009 Ohio 3640 (Ohio Ct. App. 2009).

Hornoff, Jeffrey Scott

Douglas Hadden, *Man to be Freed on Murder Rap,* PAWTUCKET TIMES (Rhode Island), Nov. 5, 2002 *available at* http://truthinjustice.org/Hornoff_Exonerated.htm.
Hans Sherrer and Jeffrey Scott Hornoff, *Jeffrey Scott Hornoff's Murder Conviction Is Exposed as a Sham When the Real Killer Confesses,* JUSTICE DENIED, Issue 23, March 3, 2003, *available at* http://justicedenied.org/issue/issue_23/jeffrey_scott_hornoff.html.
State v. Hornoff, 1996 R.I. Super. LEXIS 124, *1 (R.I. Super. Ct. 1996).

Howard, Tim

Centurion Ministries, Friends and Benefactors Letters, June 11, 2003, http://www.centurionministries.org/letters-061103.html.
State v. Howard, 383 N.E2d 912 (Ohio 1978).
Alan Johnson, *$1.5 Million for Freed Man; Settlement Finishes Case of 2 Innocent Men who Spent Decades in Prison,* COLUMBUS DISPATCH (Columbus, Ohio), May 18, 2007, at 01B.

Hunt, Lee Wayne

Information on file with Richard Rosen, Professor, University of North Carolina School of Law.
State v. Hunt, 381 S.E.2d 453, 455 (N.C. 1989).

Keine, Ron

Larry King Live, *Death Penalty Trial,* (CNN television broadcast aired December 21, 2004) (transcript available at http://www.ronkeine.org/CNN.html).
LESLIE LYTLE, EXECUTION'S DOORSTEP: TRUE STORIES OF THE INNOCENT AND NEAR DAMNED 1-3, 19-22 (Northeastern University Press 2008).
Witness to Innocence, *Ron Keine,* http://witnesstoinnocence.org/view_stories.php?Ron-Keine-24 (last visited Nov. 27, 2010).

Killian, Gloria

Henry Weinstein, *Conviction for Murder Reversed Appeal: Justices Find in Favor of Ex-Law Student Who has Served 16 Years of her Sentence for Plotting Robbery, Slaying,* L.A. TIMES, March 14, 2002, at Cal. Metro part 2, pg. 1, *available at* http://articles.latimes.com/2002/mar/14/local/me-perjury14.

Krone, Ray

The Innocence Project, *Ray Krone,* http://www.innocenceproject.org/Content/Ray_Krone.php (last visited Nov. 27, 2010).

Lamb, Larry
Information on file with Christine Mumma, Director, North Carolina Center on Actual Innocence.

Lomax, Walter
Julie Bykowicz, *Man is Set Free After 39 Years Behind Bars,* BALTIMORE SUN, Dec. 14, 2006, at 1A.
Centurion Ministries, http://www.centurionministries.org (last visited Nov. 27, 2010).
Centurion Ministries, *Walter Lomax,* http://www.centurionministries.org (follow "Cases" hyperlink; then choose "Walter Lomax" from the drop down menu).
Lomax v. Warden, Md. Corr. Training Ctr., 741 A.2d 476, 478 (Md. 1999).

Macumber, Bill
Newsworthy Developments: The Macumber Case, JUST. PROJECT Q. Volume 1, Issue 1, at 4, *available at* http://www.azjusticeproject.org/Assets/newsletter/jp_quarterly_01.pdf (last visited Nov. 27, 2010).

McClendon, Robert
The Innocence Project, *Robert McClendon,* http://www.innocenceproject.org/Content/Robert_McClendon.php (last visited Nov. 27, 2010).

Monroe, Beverly
Mid-Atlantic Innocence Project, *Beverly Monroe,* http://www.exonerate.org/case-profiles/beverly-monroe/ (last visited Nov. 27, 2010).
Monroe v. Angelone, 323 F.3d 286 (4th Cir. 2003).
Monroe v. Angelone, 2002 U.S. Dist. LEXIS 26310 (E.D. Va. Mar. 28, 2002).

Piaskowski, Mike
DENIS GULLICKSON AND JOHN GAIE, THE MONOFILS CONSPIRACY 1-5 (iUniverse.com 2009).
Piaskowski v. Bett, 256 F.3d 687 (7th Cir. 2001).

Rafay, Atif
Appeal Campaign for Atif Rafay and Sebastian Burns, Facts of the Case, http://rafayburnsappeal.com/facts.html (last visited Nov. 27, 2010).
Appeal Campaign for Atif Rafay and Sebastian Burns, The Mr. Big Strategy, http://www.rafayburnsappeal.com/falseconfessions.html (last visited Nov. 27, 2010).
Appeal Campaign for Atif Rafay and Sebastian Burns, Timeline, http://www.rafayburnsappeal.com/timeline.html (last visited Nov. 27, 2010).

Rea, Julie
Downstate Illinois Innocence Project, *The Julie Rea-Harper Case,* http://www.uis.edu/innocenceproject/ (follow "Exonerees" hyperlink; then follow "Julie Rea-Harper" hyperlink) (last visited Nov. 27, 2010).

Smith, Kalvin Michael
Dan Galindo, *Judge Rejects Plea, Smith Will Not Get a New Trial,* WINSTON-SALEM JOURNAL (North Carolina), January 9, 2009, at Local A1.
Gergely Kanicska, *Students Investigate Plausible Claims of Wrongful Convictions,* DUKE LAW MAGAZINE, Fall 2005, *available at* http://www.law.duke.edu/magazine/2005fall/features/innocenceindex.html.
Phoebe Zerwick, *It Takes A Village to Work for Justice,* DUKE LAW MAGAZINE, Summer 2009, *available at* http://www.law.duke.edu/magazine/2009summer/feature/index.
Phoebe Zerwick, *Part One: The Crime,* WINSTON-SALEM JOURNAL, (North Carolina), *available at* http://silkplantforest.journalnow.com/articles/part01/article/ (last visited Nov. 27, 2010).
Phoebe Zerwick, *Part Two: The Case,* WINSTON-SALEM JOURNAL, (North Carolina), *available at* http://silkplantforest.journalnow.com/articles/part02/article/ (last visited Nov. 27, 2010).
Phoebe Zerwick, *Part Three: The Confession,* WINSTON-SALEM JOURNAL, (North Carolina), *available at* http://silkplantforest.journalnow.com/articles/part03/ (last visited Nov. 27, 2010).

Smith, Nancy
John Caniglia, *Nancy Smith, Joseph Allen Acquitted by Lorain County Judge in Head Start Sex Abuse Case after Serving 14 Years in Prison,* THE PLAIN DEALER (Cleveland, Ohio), June 25, 2009, B1.
Ohio Innocence Project, *Nancy Smith and Joseph Allen – Exonerated June 2009,* http://www.law.uc.edu/institutes-centers/ohio-innocence-project/significant-cases/nancy-smith-and-joseph-allen (last visited Nov. 27, 2010).
Mark Puente, *Doubts Linger Years After Lorain Head Start Sex Trial,* THE PLAIN DEALER (Cleveland, Ohio), June 14, 2009, A6.
State v. Smith, 2010 Ohio 3007, at *P2-*P4, (Ohio Ct. App. 2010).

Towler, Raymond
Innocence Project, *Raymond Towler,* http://www.innocenceproject.org/Content/Raymond_Towler.php (last visited Nov. 27, 2010).

Townsend, Sherman
Robert Downs, *Innocence and the Justice System,* MINNESOTA DAILY, Dec. 8, 2009, *available at* http://www.mndaily.com/2009/12/08/innocence-and-justice-system (last visited Nov. 27, 2010).
David Hanners, *St. Paul Man Freed After 10 Years; Judge Commutes His Sentence in Burglary Case,* PIONEER PRESS (St. Paul, Minnesota), Oct. 2, 2007 *available at* http://truthinjustice.org/sherman-townsend.htm

PART THREE / THE INNOCENTS

ACKNOWLEDGEMENTS

This project would not have been possible without the support of many people including (in alphabetical order)

Shawn Armbrust Executive Director, Mid-Atlantic Innocence Project

Adele Bernhard Pace Law School Post-Conviction Project

Louis D. Bilionis Dean and Nippert Professor of Law, University of Cincinnati College of Law

Dan Bolick

Stan Brod Adjunct Professor, College of Design, Art, Architecture and Planning and the students in his Fall 2010 Design Methodology class including:

Samantha Anthony
Sarah Carne
Melissa Chavez
Caroline Ferneding
Laura Frycek
Jessica Hoh
Joey Howell
Tim Huff
Cami Huntington
Anne Koch
Nicci Martinez
Alicia Meldrum
Lauren Oka
Kim Pieper
Jenny Price
Tyler Rice
Jamie Ritzer
Bethany Taylor
Amy Vanderbur
Izzie Zahorian

The *Freedom Center Journal* Staff p. 3

Lawrence Golden Director, Downstate Illinois Innocence Project, University of Illinois at Springfield

Greg Hampikian Director of the Idaho Innocence Project, Boise State University

Michael Hogan Associate Director, Development, University of Cincinnati College of Law

Sean Hughes Assistant Professor of Journalism and the Photojournalism and Design Coordinator and students in his Photojournalism Workshop course including **Lisa Haynes-Henry,** Graduate Student in Professional Writing and Editing and **Sam Spencer,** Senior Photojournalism Major

The Innocence Project

Julie Jonas Managing Attorney, Innocence Project of Minnesota

Lisa Kurtz Assistant to the Executive Director, Centurion Ministries

Kathryn Monroe Director, Rocky Mountain Innocence Center

Christine Mumma Director, North Carolina Center on Actual Innocence

The Ohio Innocence Project Staff p. 5, and a special thank you to **Amanda Rieger**

Adrian Parr Associate Professor, Department of Women's Gender and Sexuality Studies, and the School of Architecture and Interior Design, University of Cincinnati

Katherine Puzauskas Case and Programs Coordinator, Arizona Justice Project

Richard Rosen Professor, University of North Carolina School of Law

Lois and Dick Rosenthal

Peggy Ruwe Development Coordinator, University of Cincinnati College of Law

Ann and Harry Santen

James J. Schoenfeld Assistant Dean, Administration and Finance, University of Cincinnati College of Law

Karen Sieber Senior Director, Development, University of Cincinnati College of Law

Taryn Simon

Witness to Innocence

Joe York University of Mississippi